CW00684010

CONTENTS

Ships in Focus Publications

Correspondence and editorial:
Roy Fenton
18 Durrington Avenue
London SW20 8NT
0181 879 3527
rfenton@rfenton.demon.co.uk

Orders and photographic:
John & Marion Clarkson
18 Franklands, Longton
Preston PR4 5PD
01772 612855

Printed by Amadeus Press Ltd., Huddersfield.
Designed by Hugh Smallwood, John Clarkson and Roy Fenton.
SHIPS IN FOCUS RECORD
ISBN 0 9521179 9 1

SHIPS IN FOC

To fleet list or not to fleet li
occupying the minds of your e
formalised listings of the dimensions, machinery, builders and careers of ships belonging to a company or class. Let it be said that we regard the fleet list as one of the enduring gifts made to the enthusiast by the World Ship Society, whose publications have developed the format over the years. As a way of giving a ship's particulars and history in a concise and familiar format, they are unparalleled, and have a flexibility which allows much additional data to be accommodated. They also suit our avowed intent to provide essential details of the ships which we feature in *Record*. However, they do not make the easiest read, and their appeal is mainly to those who want a permanent record of a ship. Our view is that there is an important place for fleet lists in *Record*, especially of ships which had complex careers, but that they should not become too dominant. In this issue, at least five features could have justified accompanying fleet lists, but in several - including the *Fleet in Focus* feature on Guinness ships - we have opted to put the appropriate data into captions instead. We would be interested in further views of readers on this issue, having already received and partly responded to calls for 'more fleet lists'.

The question of binding *Record* has arisen, and we have arranged with a bookbinder whose work we trust to have them bound into volumes of four. Cloth binding with gold embossing will cost £15 including return postage to an address in the UK. Please send your copies direct to Mr. R. Smith, Nullisec, Main Road, Chattenden, Rochester, Kent ME3 8LW with cheques for £15 made payable to 'The Bindery'. We are told that orders will take approximately six weeks.

Those who read the editorial in *Record 5* carefully may wonder how we can justify the subject of Guinness as a *major* Irish Sea fleet. We have to admit that the *Fleet in Focus* feature originally planned has simply outgrown the available space, and we plan a book devoted to the company.

This brings us to some good news for *Record* subscribers: we will be offering them concessions on the price of several new books which we have in the pipeline. If you don't already subscribe, we would strongly suggest you consider doing so. In addition to this concession, subscribing also gives a saving on the postage of three issues, and ensures each *Record* arrives on your doormat just as soon as it is printed. We would remind readers that they can start their subscription with *any* issue, and are welcome to backdate it so that they receive previous copies. Subscription rates for three issues appear below.

The three yearly issues of *Record* are published early in February, June and October. Those in UK and Europe who subscribe or who have placed an order can expect to receive their copy by the end of these months: if by any chance yours fails to turn up by then, please let us know immediately.

Roy Fenton   John Clarkson
June 1998

SUBSCRIPTION RATES FOR THREE ISSUES OF *RECORD*		
UK	£20	
Europe (airmail)	£22	
Rest of world (surface mail)	£22	US$36
Rest of world (airmail)	£30	US$49

CARROWDORE

Scott and Sons, Bowling; 1914, 599gt, 180 feet

CARROWDORE was bought from John Kelly within a month of completion, before her holds were sullied with the Belfast merchants' coal. The metal beads which aided Kelly's mates in painting their owner's funnel rings were retained throughout Guinness's ownership, and proved useful to CARROWDORE's final owner. For after a remarkable 39 years with Guinness, including two world wars, she returned to the coal trade in 1953 for Arthur S. Davidson Ltd. of Belfast. Continuing under the name Kelly had chosen back in 1914 she carried on steaming across the Irish Sea until 1958 when, on 25th November, she arrived at Boom near Antwerp to be broken up by Van den Bossche and Company. *[World Ship Photo Library]*

CLARECASTLE

Scott and Sons, Bowling; 1914, 627gt, 180 feet

CLARECASTLE was a sister to CARROWDORE, and their careers ran almost exactly in parallel. Guinness bought her early in 1915 - she was the only one of the three ex-Belfast colliers to have run for John Kelly - and after sale to Davidson in 1953 she lasted until 1958, arriving at Irvine on 10th December to be demolished by the Ayrshire Dockyard Co. Ltd. The reason for her being dressed overall in this view is not known.
[World Ship Photo Library]

Fleet in Focus:
GUINNESS

Even if it can no longer be claimed that 'Guinness is good for you', there is no doubt that the bitter stout has been very good indeed for the Irish economy. Next to cattle, the product of the St. James' Gate Brewery may well have been the largest commodity exported from the island, certainly during the nineteenth century. The use of sea transport across the Irish Sea has been at the heart of Guinness's success.

Arthur Guinness founded his brewery in 1759. At the time, most of Ireland was economically backward, to the extent that 95% of the population were living at subsistence level. The local market for Guinness's brewery was confined to the city of Dublin and its surroundings. Even here, Guinness faced strong competition from London brewers who could offer economies of scale with which the Irish brewer could not compete. The brewer's best hope was to beat the Londoners at their own game and tap into the much larger English market. Local economic factors helped Guinness in its early days. The so-called 'ascendancy', the 5% of the population which owned most of the land, controlled the Irish Parliament before the 1800 Act of Union, and the Parliament's laws tended to favour local businesses. For instance, beer tax was abolished in 1795 and Irish brewers also received protection from their competitors in the form of import duties. In addition, the inflation which affected Dublin in the last years of the eighteenth century devalued the Irish pound against the English pound and gave them a price advantage on the adjoining island. But it was excellent brewing and business skills which assured Guinness's success in the English market. One important factor was the specialisation after 1799 in just one product - porter - which because of its biological stability could be brewed in large quantities and readily exported. Another factor was the use of steam shipping to

Bristol and Liverpool from around 1822. Steady expansion saw Guinness not only come to dominate Irish brewing, but also to achieve a market penetration on the adjacent island which no English brewer has ever approached: what other beer has ever been available in almost every pub in the land? Financial success accompanied sales success, and the 1886 flotation of Arthur Guinness, Son and Co. Ltd. was greeted almost as eagerly by the stock market as some of the latter day privatisations of public utilities. During this century the company also became legendary for its successful advertising and marketing.

Guinness has long depended on sea transport, particularly to carry their stout to England, but also to bring in malting barley from Wexford and New Ross. Around the turn of the century they also began using steam barges running from the brewery to ships docking in Dublin. However, the first tentative step into shipowning was taken in 1913 when Guinness bought the W.M. BARKLEY from John Kelly. The 15-year old unmodified collier was, by some accounts, not the ideal ship to carry oak casks of beer from Dublin to Salthouse Dock, Liverpool, but nevertheless within the next two years the brewer returned to the Belfast coal merchant and bought three newly-completed colliers, CARROWDORE, CLARECASTLE and CLAREISLAND. At least two of these had refrigeration plant installed, but they remained essentially colliers, and all went back into the coal trade on their eventual sales. The Guinness ships did not escape the requisition which befell coasters during the First World War nor, with the loss of W.M. BARKLEY, the attentions of U-boats which the Royal Navy was seemingly powerless to prevent.

Continued use of the British flag for Guinness ships

W.M. BARKLEY
Ailsa Shipbuilding Co., Troon; 1898, 569g, 179 feet
Although the image of W.M. BARKLEY at Custom House Quay is thought to be unaltered, this postcard has seen some retouching, with the drawing in of Guinness steam barges which brought the stout from Victoria Wharf at the brewery itself. Bought in 1913, W.M. BARKLEY was requisitioned in 1916, carrying stone from the Channel Islands to France for roadmaking, but her owners managed to get her returned, only to lose her in the Irish Sea. The only Guinness-owned ship ever lost, W.M. BARKLEY was torpedoed and sunk by German submarine UC 75 on 12th October 1917 seven miles east of the Kish Light Vessel whilst on a voyage from Dublin to Liverpool with her usual cargo of stout. Four of her crew were lost, including the master, the other seven being rescued by the DUNNET HEAD (426/1905) and landed at Dublin.
[Terry O'Conallain]

after Irish independence in 1922 seems to have reflected the anglicisation of the Guinness family, but it was rather anomalous as the ships were managed and owned in Dublin and their crews recruited in Ireland. Independence did bring important changes, as a tariff war broke out between the Republic and the UK. To protect its British interests, Guinness set up a company registered in London, which owned the distribution machinery and later a local brewery, and marketed the product in Britain. Part of the process of consolidating the British business was the ordering of a larger, purpose-built vessel for the Dublin to London trade, the GUINNESS.

The fleet of three ships remained intact throughout the Second World War, and this time escaped requisition. This was probably part of a deal between the Irish and UK governments which allowed Irish-owned ships to bunker at British ports and receive Navicerts to permit their voyages in return for deliveries of food (and drink) from Ireland. The British Government regarded beer as being of particular importance to the nation and is known to have rejected its rationing as having a deleterious effect on morale, notwithstanding the amount of grain used in brewing which could otherwise have gone to make bread.

The CLAREISLAND had been sold on the arrival of the GUINNESS in 1931, but the two remaining colliers steamed on until 1953, and even then managed to find a Belfast owner to trade them further. Their sale by Guinness was due to the arrival of two purpose-built motorships, THE LADY GRANIA and THE LADY GWENDOLEN. Externally these appeared to be standard dry cargo coasters with a good set of cargo handling gear, but their holds were built to take circular tanks each of which carried just over 500 gallons of stout.

The GUINNESS did not achieve the longevity of the earlier colliers. By 1963 the triple-expansion steam engine was a decided anachronism, and her replacement by a motorship was no great surprise. THE LADY PATRICIA, completed in December 1962, represented a modest enlargement of the two earlier ladies, with machinery which was also by British Polar Engines Ltd. of Glasgow.

In service between Dublin and Liverpool and Manchester, the three LADYs achieved all the regularity of a liner service. Each Tuesday, one of the boats sailed from Dublin for Liverpool and one for Manchester. Thursday saw another Liverpool departure, and Saturday a Liverpool and a Manchester sailing. There was a tight schedule to maintain which was sometimes difficult in adverse weather conditions. This was apparent in perhaps the least honourable incident in Guinness's shipowning career when THE LADY GWENDOLEN ran down and sank Zillah's motorship FRESHFIELD (518/1954) in the Mersey during November 1961. At the time the FRESHFIELD was anchored in fog, yet - although he admitted that visibility was so bad that he could not see the forecastle from the bridge - the master of the Guinness boat was proceeding at his full speed of about ten knots. As justification, he claimed he had his radar set on, but it emerged that only he and the helmsman were on the bridge and that he was paying the radar scant attention. It seems THE LADY GWENDOLEN's master was in the habit of using full speed in fog in order to keep to his schedule. In the subsequent enquiry his owners were judged negligent for neither impressing on the master the proper procedures for safe navigation in fog, nor for checking that he was following these by comparing deck logs which would record that conditions were foggy with engine room records which would indicate the speed at the time.

CLAREISLAND
Scott and Sons, Bowling; 1915, 633gt, 181 feet
The third of the three Kelly sisters bought in 1914 and 1915 had the shortest career, being made redundant in 1931 when the GUINNESS was delivered. The Antrim Iron Ore Co. Ltd. of Belfast purchased CLAREISLAND and renamed her GLENDUN. On 15th February 1940 GLENDUN was wrecked near Maughold Head, Isle of Man whilst on a voyage from Garston to Belfast with a cargo of coal. Hers was one of a number of wartime casualties to which the extinguishing of lights around the Irish Sea may have contributed.

GUINNESS

Ailsa Shipbuilding Co. Ltd., Troon; 1931, 1,151g, 212 feet

The building of the GUINNESS was a bold step for the brewers at a time of economic gloom and depression, but perhaps illustrating that not all industries suffer equally at such times. Guinness would have got a good price from Ailsa who, after completing GUINNESS, built only one ship in the next three years. GUINNESS had one large, refrigerated and insulated hold suitable for carrying 800 tons of stout in oak casks. She was in all respects an excellent buy, giving service first on the

Dublin to London service, normally a 60-hour passage. Her eponymous cargoes continued to go down so well in the south of England that the company decided to open a brewery at Park Royal just to the west of London to serve the south of England, and in 1938 GUINNESS switched to the Dublin – Mersey trade, eventually running exclusively to Pomona Docks in Manchester.

Becoming very familiar in the Mersey and Manchester Ship Canal in post-war years, GUINNESS also served as an excellent reminder of the company's brand, and with

her dark blue hull she was very well kept as the photograph on the cover of this publisher's *Classic Coasters* demonstrates. Note also the harp proudly displayed on the bridge front. Her steam reciprocating engines destined her to a relatively early demise, however, and on 12th June 1963 she arrived at Faslane to be broken up by Shipbreaking Industries Ltd.

The two photographs show that GUINNESS was subtly altered during her career, with the lower showing her bridge front rebuilt and with differences in colour scheme. [Both: *World Ship Photo Library*]

The last chapter in the Guinness-by-sea saga began in 1974 when THE LADY PATRICIA was converted to a beer tanker. This experiment was successful enough to merit the ordering of a purpose-built tanker, the MIRANDA GUINNESS. The two dry cargo motor vessels were made redundant, although both found further owners. Beer was now loaded from road tankers in Dublin, via a pumproom and piping fitted on the quayside, and delivered in bulk via the Manchester Ship Canal to Wiggs Wharf near Runcorn from where it was sent to a bottling plant.

Recent years have not been very happy ones for the Guinness company, blighted by a failed and unhappy take-over attempt for the Distillers Company, and strong suggestions that this once most sure-footed of marketing organisations had lost its way. The fashion for 'concentrating on core business' has meant that shipping the product has been left to others. In 1985 Guinness handed over the management of its ships to Irish Marine Services Ltd. of Dublin, a company run largely by staff from the late-lamented Irish Shipping Ltd. The company decided to put the MIRANDA GUINNESS and THE LADY PATRICIA under the Irish flag and reregistered them in Dublin.

Political developments within the company saw Guinness cease shipowning in the early 1990s. Rivalry within the group threatened to leave the St James' Gate Brewery supplying only the Irish market, and so a further economy was instituted, that of dehydrating the stout in Dublin and shipping over a concentrate to be diluted in England. Providers of regular Irish Sea shipping services jumped at a chance to carry the cargo, and the concentrate is now shipped in liquid containers on regular Irish Sea services. THE LADY PATRICIA and MIRANDA GUINNESS became redundant and their scrapping in 1993 and 1994 saw the extinction of that rare breed of ship, the beer tanker.

With their red and black funnels, the immaculately-kept Guinness boats had been an excellent advertisement for their owner's brand for some eighty years. With their demise yet another familiar part of the Irish Sea shipping scene slipped away, leaving less trace than the froth on a glass after a pint of stout has slipped down a thirsty throat.

THE LADY GRANIA
Ailsa Shipbuilding Co. Ltd., Troon; 1953, 1,166gt, 204 feet
For almost forty years Guinness had been carried across the Irish Sea in casks. The 1950s saw interest in unit load carrying on the Irish Sea and Guinness became part of this revolution by ordering two motorships which could carry their stout in transportable tanks. Made of stainless steel and aluminium, the tanks were relatively modest in size, their 504 gallon capacity being the equivalent of 14 barrels. First of the motorships was THE LADY

GRANIA, built like her predecessor at Troon. As the July 1971 photograph shows, to outward appearances she was a conventional dry cargo coaster, with a good outfit of cargo gear. This was necessary for the large number of tanks she carried: 95 in the forward hold and 127 in the after hold. As in the GUINNESS, the holds were insulated and fitted with refrigerating equipment.

THE LADY GRANIA was made redundant by the conversion of THE LADY PATRICIA into a beer tanker in 1974. She found

owners in Halifax, Nova Scotia who traded her from Canada to the West Indies, reflecting their title, Halifax Caribbean Shipping Ltd. and her new name THE LADY SCOTIA. She retained this name through a transfer to Cayman Islands registry in 1978 which saw her trade into the Pacific and Australia, and somewhat incongruously carried it after sale in 1979 to owners in Mazatlan, Mexico. Her eventual fate is not well recorded, and all that is known is that in 1981 she went aground off Cabo San Lucas during a hurricane.

THE LADY GWENDOLEN

Ardrossan Dockyard Co. Ltd.,
Ardrossan; 1953, 1,164gt, 205 feet

The 1950s Guinness motorships very much reflected contemporary British coaster building practice. They were driven along at eleven knots by six-cylinder British Polar engines, and the satisfaction with this make is reflected in its use right up to the last Guinness ship. Each man and boy of the 14-member crew had his own cabin, although in the best traditions the master and deck officers were accommodated in the bridge, well isolated from the deck hands and engineers who lived in the poop.

THE LADY GWENDOLEN was replaced by the MIRANDA GUINNESS in 1976 and became the Piraeus-owned PAROS. On 10th November 1979 she was run down and sunk whilst at anchor in Ravenna Roads. Both of the conventional motorships thus came to violent ends.

The top photograph shows THE LADY GWENDOLEN loading stout alongside the Georgian city of Dublin's magnificent Custom House. The lower view from 1971 also shows her on the Liffey. Despite a persistent folk tale, this river is not the source of water for the Guinness brewery, but Dublin's Grand Canal, down which it flows from springs in County Kildare.
[Both: World Ship Photo Library]

THE LADY PATRICIA

Charles Hill and Sons Ltd., Bristol; 1962, 1,187gt, 213 feet

As built, THE LADY PATRICIA was a relatively modest development of the earlier motorships, designed to replace the GUINNESS. Like her forerunner, she had all her accommodation aft, a trend which became general once the crew were given decent ventilation, heating and plumbing, in that it meant providing just one set of services rather than one aft and one for the midships bridge structure. Compared to the earlier LADYs, THE LADY PATRICIA represented evolution rather than revolution, as her engine was a British Polar unit, this time of seven cylinders giving her 11.5 knots. She was built to carry the same transportable tanks as her older companions and, as the upper 1966 view shows, had two four-ton deck cranes to unload them.

A revolution did affect THE LADY PATRICIA in 1974 when she was converted to a bulk beer tanker, probably the world's first. After her deck cranes and other now superfluous equipment had been removed by the Liffey Dockyard, she went back to her Bristol builders for the major part of the conversion work, which involved fitting cylindrical tanks mounted vertically. These tanks had been proven in experiments with THE LADY GRANIA, which had them fitted into her fore hold. THE LADY PATRICIA was fitted with 16 tanks, each having a capacity of 130 barrels or 4,680 gallons, corresponding to that of the road tankers from which they loaded. A peculiar feature of the conversion was that, in spite of the cargo space being extended upwards, it was

considered necessary to raise her centre of gravity to prevent her becoming too stiff. Difficult though it might be to believe, the white structure seen raised above the deck amidships in the lower photograph is a ballast tank. The change from removable to fixed beer tanks meant that it was necessary to sterilise the cargo space and to provide the steam for this the motorship had a boiler installed. Cleaning was carried out during the homeward voyage. A bow thruster was also fitted during the period in Charles Hills' hands.

The conversion was clearly a success, as the whole of the Guinness shipments across the Irish Sea were eventually carried by tanker, giving a saving of one ship. THE LADY PATRICIA's career was undoubtedly lengthened by this conversion and she was not taken out of service until August 1991 to lay up at Dublin.

Irish Marine Services Ltd. were instructed to sell the ships they had been managing for Guinness since 1985, but the owners insisted that they were renamed. THE LADY PATRICIA became MAINE (Middle photograph) after a river in Limerick where one of Irish Marine Services directors had been brought up. On 25th November 1993 she arrived in the Manchester Ship Canal to be broken up by TMI Metals Ltd. who by March 1994 had completed demolishing her in an old dry dock in Manchester.
[Left and this page middle Les Hodder]

MIRANDA GUINNESS
Charles Hill and Sons Ltd., Bristol; 1976, 1,541gt, 71 metres
MIRANDA GUINNESS was prosaically described by *Lloyd's Register* as an 'alcohol carrier'. In a world thirsty for records - a tendency encouraged, of course, by her owner's publications - she could well have been the first (and probably the last) purpose-built beer tanker. Her Bristol builders seem likely to have won the order on the strength of their building and later converting THE LADY PATRICIA, design work being started before the conversion of the latter was completed. Sadly,

MIRANDA GUINNESS was to be the last ship from Charles Hill, their Albion Dockyard being closed down not by economic forces, but by a local authority's misguided belief that the River Avon was no longer a place for commercial shipping and shipbuilding activities.

MIRANDA GUINNESS's career was depressingly short and she was taken out of service at the age of only seventeen years. Briefly renamed MAIGUE before a sale to an Irish company who styled themselves Eriskay Ltd., her penultimate call was at Bramley Moore Dock, Liverpool

where valuable material such as her stainless steel tanks was removed. The Mersey witnessed its last movement by a Guinness boat on 12th February 1994 as MAIGUE was towed down to Garston for shipbreakers S. Evans and Sons to complete her reduction to scrap. It is hard to escape the conclusion that the ship had still much useful life in her. Her stainless steel tanks are said to have fetched as much as they cost, and the engine was taken out of the hull and is rumoured to be still earning its living in an Australian vessel. *[Paul Boot]*

THE PORT OF BARROW-IN-FURNESS
Part One
Edward Paget-Tomlinson

Early days

Along with the industrialisation of Britain during the nineteenth century went urbanisation on an ever increasing scale. This could reach dramatic proportions as, for instance, in the case of Middlesbrough, the creation of the Stockton & Darlington Railway, non-existent before 1830, but by 1880 a major port and industrial centre; while on the west coast was another railway inspired town which also started from nothing: Barrow-in-Furness.

Forming the western arm of Morecambe Bay the Furness peninsula was, in the early nineteenth century, remote and thinly populated with Ulverstone (then spelt with an 'e') the only centre of any size. At the tip of the peninsula, facing Walney Island, was the hamlet of Barrowhead or Barrow. The only port in the area, if port it could be called, was the deep-water anchorage of Piel to the south of Barrowhead, protected by the peninsula and the southern end of Walney. This had been used for the trade of Furness Abbey, the great Cistercian monastery founded in 1127, whose monks developed a considerable commercial enterprise embracing farm produce and timber extraction. Cargoes were loaded and landed here, and even Barrow itself is mentioned as early as 1396, not admittedly as a port but as a right of way. Piel Castle on Foulney Island guarding the anchorage was built as a fortified warehouse, wood at first, but later stone; the present buildings date from the early fourteenth century. In 1720 the anchorage had become busy enough to warrant a Customs House, built that year, but later this was moved to the rising port of Ulverstone. Iron ore and smelted iron were the main commodities shipped, with carts coming down to various points on the Furness shore including Barrow, sheltered by Barrow Island. More positive evidence of maritime activity at Barrow comes later in the eighteenth century with the Backbarrow Company sending down ore in 1745 and by 1776, certainly, stockpiling it at Barrow for shipment. Founded in 1711 the Backbarrow Company had a furnace on the banks of the Leven about two miles south of its outfall from Lake Windermere, which remained at work until 1967. In the early 1780s another smelting company built a quay at Barrow which was in use by 1782 with ships loading locally mined ore. This was the Newland Company founded in 1747 which had a furnace near Ulverston which can still be seen. Ulverston was the main port of Furness at this time, its importance much enhanced by the completion of the ship canal up to the town in 1796, but already Barrow was beginning to provide competition with its ore traffic as did Kirkby on the Duddon Estuary side of Furness with the export of slates from the quarries above the village.

The Furness Railway

Piel was considered important enough to be provided with a lighthouse at the south end of Walney in 1790 and, to jump ahead a few decades, Barrow important enough to be given three more cargo jetties during the period from 1832 to 1839. A final jetty was built by Henry Schneider, of whom more later, in 1842, a date well within the railway age and railways were indeed to be the key to the future of Barrow. As a harbour Barrow had the advantage of shelter by Barrow Island and the ten miles of Walney Island but the disadvantage of a considerable tidal range, strong currents and scour with a constantly changing pattern of shoals, so that maintaining any kind of scheduled sailings was not possible. For the ore traffic a timetable was not important, but of real concern was Barrow's isolation from the main industries and communications of the rest of the British Isles. Until the 1840s the port could only depend on local traffic but the coming of the railways would soon overcome this difficulty. The first railway in Furness was as local as the horse-drawn carts which it replaced, but the merits of expansion soon became apparent. Incorporated in 1844 and completed in 1846, the Furness Railway was an isolated mineral line built to bring ore from the mines at Dalton and slates from the Kirkby quarries down to Barrow, with a branch to Piel Pier on Roa Island, serving the established deepwater anchorage, unaffected by tide and current. The Piel Pier branch was the last section of line to be opened, in August 1846, leading onto the causeway which linked Roa Island 'to the neighbouring island of Great Britain' as the London banker John Abel Smith put it. Abel Smith had bought Roa Island some years previously, envisaging a steamer service across Morecambe Bay from Fleetwood as part of a sea-cum-rail route to the north, with the Preston & Wyre Railway providing the Fleetwood connection and the Furness Railway a possible extension to Carlisle and Scotland. Under an Act of 1843 Abel Smith had built both the causeway and pier, the Furness Railway simply provided the rails.

Abel Smith also had the idea of creating a harbour company based on Roa Island with a wide authority over the landing places of the district, but all he actually achieved were his causeway and pier, which the Furness Railway were forced to use on his terms, as passenger services with rail connections needed access to the pier at any state of the tide to keep to a timetable. With the railway open to Piel Pier the Fleetwood service could start, albeit shakily, with a chartered vessel, but it was an improvement on the hazardous crossing of the sands from Ulverston by coach. The Furness Railway Amendment Act of 1848, sanctioning the service, allowed the Railway Company to operate the steamer, an important step

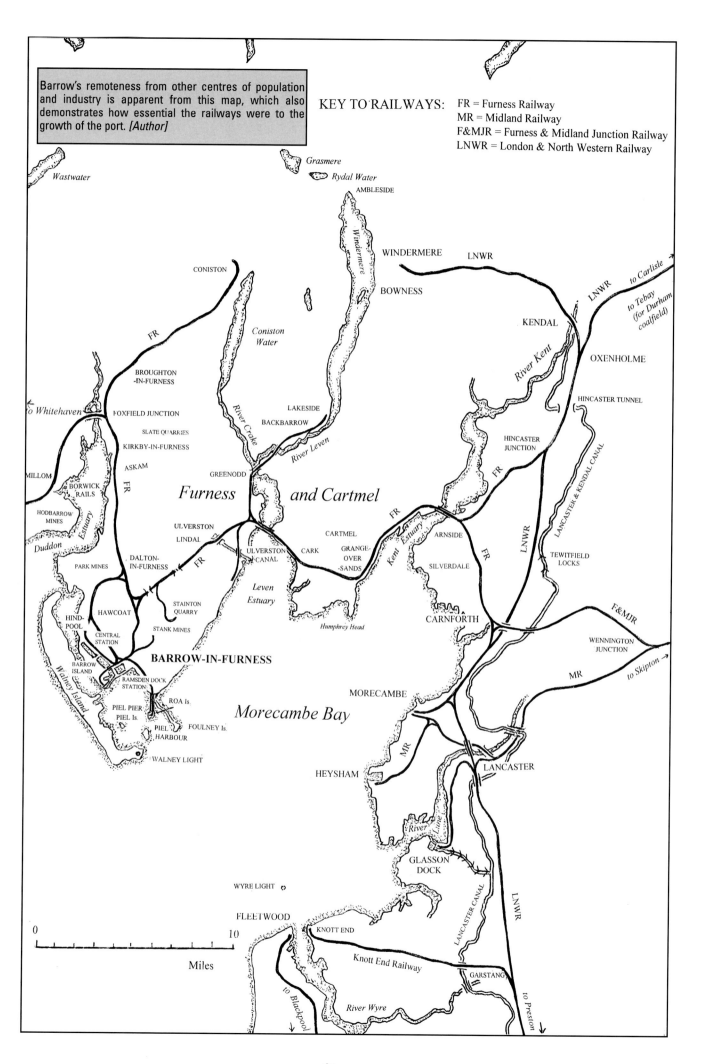

Barrow's remoteness from other centres of population and industry is apparent from this map, which also demonstrates how essential the railways were to the growth of the port. *[Author]*

KEY TO RAILWAYS:
FR = Furness Railway
MR = Midland Railway
F&MJR = Furness & Midland Junction Railway
LNWR = London & North Western Railway

forward but only made because the steamer was regarded as an integral part of the railway. It would be some years before railways would be allowed to run ships, save through nominees. Fortunately for the Furness Railway, who were having a difficult time dealing with Abel Smith, a storm damaged both Smith's pier and the causeway and in 1853 the Furness Railway were able to buy him out. Their steamer, the HELVELLYN (153gt), bought in 1847 from the Clyde, remained on the Fleetwood-Piel service until 1867. The other steamer involved was the JAMES DENNISTOUN, a Clyde-built wooden paddler of only 70 gross tons and built in 1836.

The port

There had been proposals for a Barrow Harbour Company when the jetties were built in the 1830-1840 period, at the same time as a tramway was suggested from Barrow to the mines, but ideas for the port took a more concrete form with the establishment of Commissioners for Barrow Harbour under an Act of 1848, in other words Barrow became an official port with a harbourmaster and buoyage, and later, in 1854, a steam tug was put in service. Indeed, the port was served by resident tugs, provided by its various owners from these early days until 1973 and now in 1998, after a 25-year gap, the current owners have introduced a new tug/work boat named FURNESS ABBEY.

Nominally independent under the Act, the Commissioners were in fact subservient to the Furness Railway, while for customs purposes Barrow remained an outport of Lancaster until 1872, when Barrow was allowed its own customs authority. This may sound contradictory since a Customs House for the Piel anchorage had been built in 1720, but Lancaster had always maintained the over-riding customs direction.

In the 1840s the port of Barrow existed on a very small scale, seeing only schooners and ketches whose cargo work was hindered by the great rise and fall of the tide, likewise it supported a small community, 150 people only in 1848. But it was growing fast, with well over 600 inhabitants two years later, for as an ore shipping port it was becoming increasingly important, with, by the 1850s, between 2,000 to 3,000 tons going out each week. The advantage of the railway was becoming strikingly apparent and by 1854 ore was being sent by screw steamer to South Wales on a regular basis.

This was ore of the highest quality, haematite of exceptional richness, with the added advantage of a negligible phosphorus content, a quality which was essential to the success of the first Bessemer process of steel making, patented in 1855. In 1859 haematite of this nature had been discovered at Park near Dalton-in-Furness by the mining entrepreneur H.W. Schneider and his partners. It proved to be a deposit of immense size and nine years later the ironworks of Schneider & Hannay were established at Barrow to smelt this ore. 1859 indeed could be the year of Barrow's birth as a centre of industry and as a town, for many workers now came to find employment, notably from South Staffordshire. By 1861 the population had risen to over 3,000. The ironworks were built at Hindpool, close to Barrow, on Furness Railway land and eventually became known as the Barrow Haematite Steel Company, the largest steelworks in the world at that time with, by 1871, 16 blast furnaces, 18 Bessemer converters and three 700 feet long sheds incorporating the steel making plant, three rolling mills for the production of railway lines, a plate mill, and a tyre mill.

To keep pace with this kind of industrial expansion both the railway system and the port had to be developed: indeed the steelworks could not have grown without them. Plans for harbour enlargement started in 1861 when Schneider and Robert Hannay had only three furnaces in blast at Hindpool. The Furness Railway were now the promoters of a scheme to build docks at Barrow, essential because the existing harbour dried out at low water, and their consulting engineer J.R. McClean drew up a scheme for presentation to Parliament. This had to be a railway venture, as the Furness Railway Company's chairman, the seventh Duke of Devonshire, put it: 'If the docks are not constructed by the Railway Company there is not much chance of any other parties constructing them'. But the Furness Railway did hope for support from the more powerful Midland Railway since by 1861 the Midland was a possible neighbour of the Furness; for in 1857 the Ulverston & Lancaster Railway, worked by the Furness Railway who took over the Ulverston & Lancaster in 1863, had reached the West Coast main line at Carnforth. Then in 1861 a railway from Barnard Castle reached the line to Carlisle at Tebay, which meant that coke from the Durham coalfield, essential for the production of iron and steel, could now reach Barrow by a reasonably direct route. The Midland came into the picture because in 1859 they had leased a line from Skipton to Lancaster but as yet had no connection with the Furness system. Such a connection was now planned by means of a branch from Wennington on the Skipton-Lancaster line, to Carnforth, giving the Midland access to the Furness Railway and, the Furness hoped, the opportunity to co-operate in the development of the port.

For the Midland, Barrow had the advantage of being nearer to Ireland, and promised the likelihood of better port facilities than the Midland's current maritime outlet at Morecambe, while for the Furness, the Midland connection would allow Barrow ore and pig iron to go direct to the furnaces at Sheffield. The Act for the Wennington-Carnforth line, the Furness and Midland Junction Railway, was passed in 1863 and the line opened in 1867. 1863 was also the year of the passage through Parliament of the Furness Railways's Act for Barrow's harbour, not without opposition from the historic port of Lancaster and from Lord Lonsdale who owned the ore shipping port of Borwick Rails on the Duddon, hard by the country's premier haematite mine, Hodbarrow.

Building the docks

Whereas detailed planning for the port of Barrow had been started in 1861, the vision of a great dock system had been advanced as early as 1854 by the Secretary and General Manager of the Furness

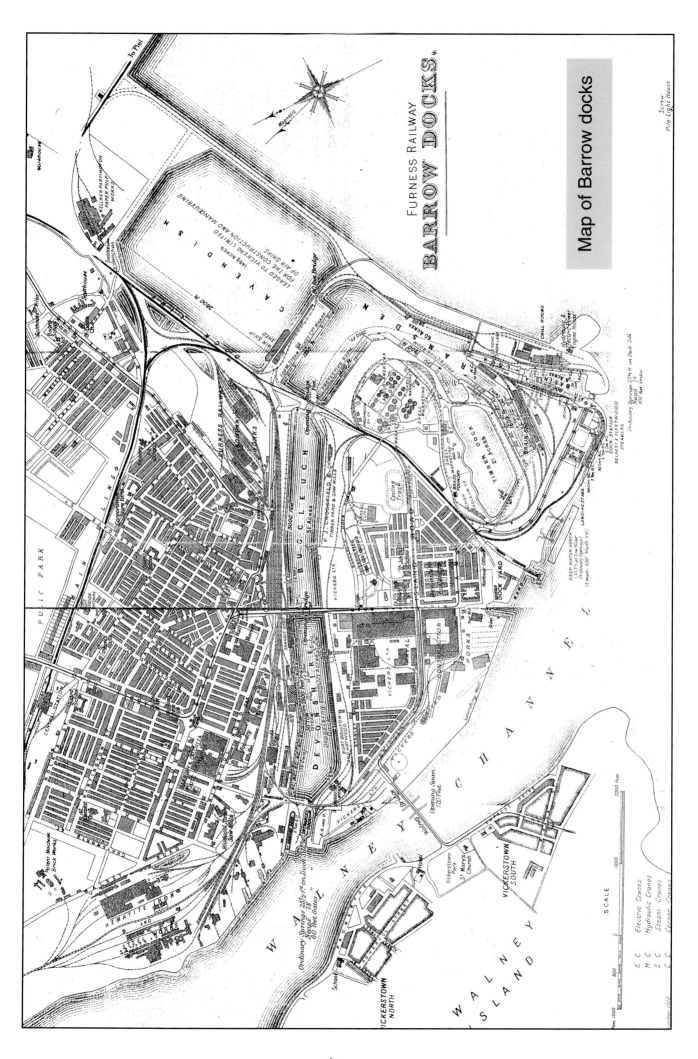

Map of Barrow docks

Railway, James Ramsden. Nobly supported by the Duke of Devonshire, Ramsden became the most insistent and persuasive promoter of Barrow in all its aspects, the port, the town, the industry, and the railway. He is indeed the founding father of Barrow. Ramsden's idea was for rail-served docks making use of the channel between Barrow and Barrow Island, for nature had done most of the excavation and all that was needed was to wall up the channel ends, a comparatively cheap task. Even so the contractor, Thomas Brassey, lost money on the undertaking because he undercut the other tenders to secure the work. Two docks, to be named after the Dukes of Devonshire and Buccleuch, were proposed within the confines of the channel and the first to be opened was the Devonshire, completed in 1867, the same year that Barrow became a municipality with James Ramsden as the first mayor. Such were the demands of shipping that the dock was brought into use before the official opening by the Duke of Devonshire. The ceremony, on 19th September 1867, was attended by the Prime Minister, W.E. Gladstone, who remarked that: 'some day Barrow will become a Liverpool. Let it become a Liverpool if it will and can, the old Liverpool will be none the worse, but better for it'. The Duke of Devonshire's most significant contribution to the rise of Barrow must be his great sense of responsibility. As a major local landowner he took his duties seriously and invested heavily to promote local industry. The rewards were often considerable but he was not afraid to support ailing ventures to keep people in work.

The second dock, the Buccleuch, was enclosed in 1868 but not ready for shipping until 1873. Along with the Duke of Devonshire, the Duke of Buccleuch had considerable estates in the area and like Devonshire was involved in industrial promotion at Barrow, lending his name and providing capital, but he had not the personal interest which characterised the attitude of his fellow peer. The two docks impounded a total of 63.5 acres of water, 32.5 in the Devonshire Dock and 31 in the Buccleuch, and construction had been a straightforward task which employed 2,000 men using locally-quarried red sandstone from Hawcoat, on the outskirts of Barrow, to build and face the dock walls. The system was entered from the north end, into Devonshire Dock, an entrance which needed constant dredging because of the scour of the tide, an expensive and never-ending problem for the port. The offices of the harbourmaster and his staff were built close to the entrance.

Ramsden and the Furness Railway hoped now for a great influx of trade, a second Liverpool, the local press describing Barrow as likely to be the best port between the Mersey and the Clyde, with shipbuilding

Two shots of the High Level Bridge between Devonshire and Buccleuch Docks show it, above, in place and, below, drawn back to admit a small steamer. Also in these views are one of the topsail schooners for which Barrow was famous.
[G. Hulme and Ken Norman collections]

and ship repairing expected as parallel developments. It was thought that shipbuilding would be well suited to the Walney Channel side of Barrow Island, prophetic views indeed. Hitherto there had been only one yard, Ashburner's, founded in 1847, which built schooners for the coastal trade, for Ulverston was the major shipbuilding centre, with the canal lined by berths.

Timber, steel and jute

Timber imports from Canada became encouraging, unloaded and stacked on the Barrow Island side of the Devonshire and Buccleuch Docks and also left to season in a timber pond at Salthouse on the south-east side of the town. Barrow's population now rocketed from 3,135 in 1861 to between 14,000 and 16,000 ten years later. In 1873 shipping movements for the year totalled 3,845, admittedly only one eighth of those at Liverpool but still impressive for a young port, even though the average size of a ship using Barrow was only half the Liverpool average. In other words, Barrow was a small scale port, welcoming schooners, ketches and barques rather than deep sea screw steamers. Apart from timber there was not so much foreign trade as expected, although the timber traffic was sufficiently impressive to encourage the big Grimsby and Gloucester timber merchants, Potter, Walker, to establish a yard at Barrow. Warehouses were built for general and bonded goods, but the cargoes that arrived were quite lost in them. The only other traffic of note was the export of steel rails from the works at Hindpool, the production of which had reached its height by the mid 1870s, coupled with ore and pig iron cargoes outward, although by this time Spanish ore was coming in to supplement local haematite. By 1878 technical improvements in steel-making processes made it possible to use ores with a higher phosphorus content, so lower grade varieties were acceptable.

Jute was another import, for the local mills established in 1870, their creation encouraged by the opening of the Suez Canal the previous year which made trade from Calcutta both easier and cheaper. They too provided much-needed employment for the women of the town. However, the history of the Barrow Flax and Jute Company was to be chequered with the Duke of Devonshire having to bail out the company with fresh capital to keep it working even at a loss.

Railway steamers

Midland Railway involvement at Barrow was limited to the use of Piel Pier for Belfast and Isle of Man steamers which moved there from Morecambe in 1867, on completion of the Wennington-Carnforth railway line. Although successful in 1848 in obtaining powers to operate ships, the Furness Railway were unable to secure a similar concession twenty years later, so the Barrow Steam Navigation Company, a consortium of Midland and Furness Railway directors together with the shipping agents James Little and Co. of Glasgow, was formed to run the services. Piel remained the terminal until 1881 when a new station was opened facing the Walney Channel by the Ramsden Dock entrance, more conveniently reached by rail. James Little first appeared as a steamship agent in 1819 and his company had a further Barrow connection when it joined with the Anchor Line of Glasgow in 1871 to begin a direct Glasgow-Barrow service with three ships, one of which was the DOM PEDRO (292/1856). The Barrow Steam Navigation Company made use of ships from the Midland Railway's Morecambe route and from the Clyde; however, further tonnage was acquired from G. & J. Burns, from the South Eastern Railway and from the London, Brighton & South Coast Railway. Sailings were by day to Douglas and Belfast and the 'Barrow route' was improved when two twin-screw ships were built for the company, the CITY OF BELFAST (1,055/1893) and the DUCHESS OF DEVONSHIRE (1,265/1897). The first came from Laird's at Birkenhead, the second from Barrow. In 1904 when

The Barrow S.N. Co. paddle steamer DUCHESS OF BUCCLEUCH alongside the station at the Ramsden Dock deep water berth which was opened in 1881. Furness Railway steamers sailing to Fleetwood and Morecambe also used this berth. Note the hydraulic crane of a type characteristic to Barrow. *[Ken Norman collection]*

MANXMAN (top)

Robert Duncan and Co., Port Glasgow; 1870, 797gt, 267 feet

The Barrow Steam Navigation Company dates from 1867 when directors of the Furness and Midland Railways - which could not obtain powers to operate steamers - joined with shipping agents James Little and Co. The company's first new paddle steamer was the ANTRIM, named for the Barrow to Belfast service, but which became MANXMAN following transfer to Douglas sailings. She is seen here leaving Maryport on what must be a festive occasion judging by the flags and onlookers lining the breakwater. MANXMAN was broken up by T.W. Ward Ltd. at Preston in 1903. *[Miss Annie Robinson MBE]*

CITY OF BELFAST (above)

Laird Brothers, Birkenhead; 1893, 1,055gt, 281 feet

CITY OF BELFAST was the first screw steamer built for the Barrow Steam Navigation Company. The Barrow fleet was sold to the Midland Railway in 1906, and the Belfast and Isle of Man sailings were transferred to Heysham. Here CITY OF BELFAST is approaching Douglas in railway company colours of red funnel with white band and black top. After war service as an armed boarding vessel, she returned to the railway services until sold to Piraeus owners in 1925. She ran in the Aegean as NICOLAOS TOGIAS until broken up in 1932. *[Ambrose Greenway collection]*

DUCHESS OF DEVONSHIRE (opp. page top)

Naval Armament and Construction Co., Barrow; 1897, 1,265gt, 300 feet

This fine-looking steamer was built for the Barrow Steam Navigation Company, being used for day sailings to the Isle of Man in summer and night sailings to Belfast for the rest of the year. Her looks were matched by her longevity, and she remained on the Heysham sailings of the Midland Railway and its successor the LMS until 1926, with a break for First World War service as an armed boarding vessel. In 1928 she was sold to Gibraltar and as GIBEL DERSA was put on sailings to Tangier. These ended in 1940, when she began a long period of inactivity which ended in a Malaga scrapyard in 1949. *[Ambrose Greenway collection]*

DUCHESS OF BUCCLEUCH (left and below)
Fairfield Shipbuilding and Engineering Co. Ltd., Govan; 1888, 838gt, 250 feet
DUCHESS OF BUCCLEUCH rolls slightly as she approaches Douglas on one of her sailings from Barrow (left). The paddler was built as ROUEN for the Newhaven to Dieppe service of the London, Brighton and South Coast Railway Company and was acquired by James Little on behalf of the Barrow Steam Navigation Company in 1903. In both views she is in the Barrow company's yellow funnel, which she retained until sold to the Midland Railway in 1906. Although of no great age, DUCHESS OF BUCCLEUCH was sold for scrap in 1910 to the Shipbreaking Co. Ltd.
[Ambrose Greenway collection]

Heysham Harbour was opened, the Midland Railway transferred the Belfast and Douglas sailings to the new port, leaving only a token service from Barrow. In 1907 even this was discontinued as the remaining vessels were absorbed into the Midland fleet operating out of Heysham, thus bringing to an end regular sailings to Belfast and the Isle of Man.

Ramsden Dock station also handled a new kind of sailing to Fleetwood in connection with Lake District tourism. The arrival of Alfred Aslett as General Manager of the Furness Railway, in succession to Sir James Ramsden (knighted in June 1872), ushered in a new approach to passenger traffic. The potentials of tourism had already been appreciated in a small way but Aslett organised excursions on a large scale with the day tripper in mind. A prime source of these was Blackpool, and he was quick to revive the old

Fleetwood-Barrow sailings with new tonnage, or at least tonnage that was designed for excursion sailings that was new to the Furness Railway. First came the LADY EVELYN (230/1900), built for the Furness Railway; then the LADY MARGARET (369/1896) was bought second-hand in 1903. When Barrow-Morecambe sailings were added, more passenger capacity was needed: first the tug, WALNEY (185/1904), which was often grossly overcrowded, then came the LADY EVELYN, followed in 1908 by PHILOMEL (564/1889) bought second-hand to replace the LADY MARGARET which had been sold. Finally GWALIA came from the Barry Railway to become LADY MOYRA (562/1905) to replace the PHILOMEL when she was scrapped. The 'Barrow Boats' tours were a huge success, but the outbreak of war in 1914 put an end to them and they were never revived.

Furness Railway steamers

LADY EVELYN (above)
J. Scott and Co., Kinghorn; 1900, 295gt, 170 feet (342g, 200 feet after 1904).
LADY EVELYN was built for the Furness Railway service across Morecambe Bay from Fleetwood to Barrow which carried trippers from Blackpool to view the Lake District. This service prospered, and in 1904 the paddler was lengthened to provide room for a further hundred passengers. As with so many other institutions, these sailings were ended by the outbreak of war in 1914. After service as a minesweeper, LADY EVELYN was sold to Cardiff owners, but ended up on the English Channel as BRIGHTON BELLE. The Second World War saw her once more requisitioned as a minesweeper, but she was unlucky during the Dunkirk evacuations and sank after striking a mine on 28th May 1940. *[Ambrose Greenway collection]*

PHILOMEL (opposite page top)
J. Scott and Co., Kirkcaldy; 1889, 564gt, 236 feet
PHILOMEL is seen here on the Thames during her ownership by the General Steam Navigation Company. She was one of a group of five excursion vessels which were the first to be given buff rather than black funnels. In 1907 she was acquired by the Furness Railway Company for their Barrow to Fleetwood service. She cost the railway £6,000: a high price for an 18-year old paddler, and something of a contrast to the £1,950 which was all the railway company got for her six years later when they sold her to T.W. Ward Ltd., who broke her up at Preston. *[World Ship Photo Library]*

LADY MOYRA (opposite page middle and bottom)
John Brown and Co., Clydebank; 1905, 562gt, 245 feet
LADY MOYRA was the last paddle steamer acquired by the Furness Railway: until 1910 she had run excursions out of Barry as GWALIA. From then her experience was uncannily like that of LADY EVELYN, with minesweeping duties followed by a short spell on the Bristol Channel and subsequent transfer to the South Coast for P. and A. Campbell as BRIGHTON QUEEN. She was even lost within three days of her former running mate, being sunk by German bombers during the Dunkirk evacuation on 1st June 1940. *[Ambrose Greenway collection]*

Problems of the port

To return to the 1870s, years of retrenchment followed the initial burst of prosperity. In 1874-5 imports dropped, to the detriment of the jute works, and the new yard of the Barrow Shipbuilding Company was not flourishing. Nevertheless work went ahead on the L-shaped Ramsden Dock and basin with one branch dock or basin, a total of 68 acres opened in 1879, with a new entrance to the docks system at the south end of the Walney Channel. A new 21-acre timber dock was created close by and Ramsden Dock was connected to the existing docks system by means of an 80-foot-wide opening into the Buccleuch Dock, crossed by a railway-carrying swing bridge. At the same time the harbour offices were moved from the north end of Devonshire Dock, close to the old entrance to the dock system, to a new building standing on a prominence near to the Ramsden Dock road. In a more optimistic atmosphere there were schemes afoot to import cattle on the hoof from the United States, and a lairage was built at the new dock. A line from New Orleans to Barrow, proposed by the Liverpool shipping company Fernies, did not materialise. Instead the Anchor Line opened a Barrow-New York service from Ramsden Dock in 1880 with their CASTALIA (2,201/1872) under the aegis of the Barrow Steamship Company. This company was founded in 1872 before the docks were fully complete as a joint venture between the Anchor Line and the Duke of Devonshire and his associates with the idea of being certain of some regular trade for the new port. Unfortunately the service, which included a call at Dublin, was short-lived: operations finished in 1881 although the berth which was used, the branch of Ramsden Dock, is known as the Anchor Line Basin to this day. Two Barrow-built ships were put on the New York service: the two-funnelled FURNESSIA (5,557/1880) and the earlier CIRCASSIA (4,272/1878).

Another venture was the Eastern Steamship Company, founded to import jute for the Barrow mills from Calcutta via the Suez Canal. The first sailing was in 1873 with the Barrow-built DUKE OF DEVONSHIRE (3,001/1873). She was to be followed by four more 'DUKES' - hence the Ducal Line title for the company. But this too was a short-lived venture, ceasing operations in 1881. The third scheme, a proposal to enter the Canadian trade by purchasing a major company, was too ambitious for a new port and never came to fruition.

One further dock, the Cavendish, was completed in 1879. Named after the famous family of which the Duke of Devonshire was the head, the Cavendish was designed for timber imports but was never used by

An aerial view from the 1930s, looking across the lock basin to the Ramsden Dock. T.W. Ward Ltd. are breaking up what appears to be a cruiser in the dock, whilst opposite this berth is a cargo steamer which may be laid up: perhaps itself awaiting scrapping. A tanker can be seen in the upper right hand corner. *[Aerofilms; Ken Norman collection]*

ships. Instead it became a timber storage pond and a reservoir for the rest of the dock system until it was leased to Vickers for the building of airships. The first British rigid airship emerged from her shed in May 1911 to lie at a mooring mast in the dock. Officially Naval Airship No. 1, she was named MAYFLY but never flew because she broke her back against the shed doors later the same year. However, a number of successful Barrow-built airships followed, culminating in 1920 with the R80 which was built not in Cavendish Dock but in a new shed on Walney Island.

By the late 1880s the docks on which Sir James Ramsden had pinned such hopes were admitted to be a failure: they were unable to support local industries such as the jute works. However, timber continued as a steady import and in 1889 a paper mill was established close to Cavendish Dock. Grain and petroleum also continued to arrive in modest quantities, and grain sheds and oil works were established at Ramsden Dock. With hindsight it is easy to see why Barrow failed to attract business. It was too far from the centres of industry: from Central Scotland; from South Lancashire, from the West Riding of Yorkshire, and from the English Midlands. Its own industries suffered for the same reason although, at the time, it was management that was blamed. Only the iron and steel works were able to sustain large import and export tonnages, and for much of the twentieth century the future of the port was dependent on the future of the blast furnaces, the Bessemer converters and the rolling mills of Hindpool. Barrow's only real advantage was its geographic proximity to Ireland and this benefited the Barrow Steam Navigation Company; its great disadvantage remained its remoteness from mainland centres of industry and population. *[To be continued]*

Ore being unloaded by a grab and bucket from a steamer in Ramsden Dock during Furness Railway days (above). The officials in the left foreground seem to be keeping their distance in the interests of the cleanliness of their straw hats. *[Ken Norman collection]*

Large buckets and hydraulic cranes were still in use at the Ramsden Dock ore berths in LMS days (below). *[Furness Museum]*

THE PALMERS OF BOSTON AND RINGASKIDDY
Gerald Lewis

The founders of many late nineteenth century shipping firms worked on the clerical side of successful shipping companies, thus learning how to operate ships at a profit before launching out into shipowning on their own account. Others were employed as master mariners, gaining a great deal of experience and making useful contacts with merchants and agents in foreign as well as home ports before purchasing old vessels at little above their scrap value, then gradually building up the fleet as the business prospered. Frederick Palmer of Boston, Lincolnshire founded a successful family shipowning business in which his son and three grandsons participated, but did not enter the world of shipping by conventional means. He had been an engine driver on the Great Northern Railway and he was 41 years of age before he began the shipping firm. His son had been apprenticed as a watchmaker and jeweller, yet together they succeeded in building up a fleet of assorted vessels which operated tenders in conjunction with the transatlantic liner companies, worked for the Government, participated in numerous salvage jobs, ran in the coastal cargo trade and operated pleasure excursions. They owned several well known vessels including the renowned tug STORMCOCK of 1877 and three former Mersey ferries.

Captain Frederick Palmer of Boston (1841-1918). *[Peter Thomas collection]*

Palmer's early career

Frederick Palmer was born on the 11th December 1841 in the village of Frithville, near Boston, Lincolnshire. He received only a basic education and at the age of 12 began work on a farm at Wrangle. In 1857 he became a locomotive cleaner with the Great Northern Railway in Boston but soon left to maintain the machinery at a local brickyard. Looking in vain for advancement in Lincoln, in 1860 he moved north and became a fitter's labourer with the Manchester, Sheffield and Lincolnshire Railway at their Sheffield depot. In 1861 he married the daughter of a local florist in Sheffield and there his son Frederick junior was born. By diligence and perseverance he rapidly improved his status and in 1864 he became an engine driver. In 1870 he transferred to the Lincoln depot and for the next fifteen years drove passenger trains.

From boyhood, Frederick Palmer had been fascinated by steam boats and whilst working on locomotive

footplates he built up and operated a service of steam packet boats on the River Witham between Lincoln and Boston and Lincoln and Gainsborough. He also became the proprietor of a jewellery business in Lincoln which was run by a manager. Frederick junior was apprenticed here as a watch maker and jeweller.

The port of Boston

Boston, one of the ports of the Hanseatic League from 1260, has seen many fluctuations in its fortunes. It saw its first steamboat when the SCOTIA (166/1828) of the St. George Steam Packet Co. began a weekly service to London in 1837. But by the early nineteenth century trade had dwindled partly due to the silting up of the river, Boston being five miles upstream from The Wash. Lack of return cargoes meant that ships bringing timber to Boston had then to sail in ballast to north east ports to load cargoes of coal for the Baltic. But the railway which connected Boston to the Nottinghamshire coalfields in 1859 encouraged the businessmen of the town to improve the state of the River Witham.

Cargoes had to be transferred from larger vessels to lighters in The Wash so in 1879, after many unsuccessful attempts, Boston Corporation reached agreement with the two major drainage authorities to drastically improve the Haven, the name given to the Witham between the town and The Wash. The following year an Act of Parliament was obtained for the construction of a dock in Boston. It was to be seven acres in extent with an entrance lock of 300 by 50 feet which was capable of accepting vessels up to 3,000 tons. The first ship in the new dock was the steamer MYRTLE (1,329/1882) which opened it on the 15th December 1884 with a cargo of cotton seed from Alexandria destined for a local mill. From 1880 until 1887 work proceeded to straighten the Haven and deepen it to 27 feet.

Palmer's Boston steamers

Frederick Palmer left the railway in 1885 and put his boyhood interest to practical use by ordering the steam screw tug MAY FLOWER from George Brown of Sculcoates on the River Hull. MAY FLOWER arrived in Boston during 1887 and Palmer used her during that summer season and the next as an excursion steamer running to Skegness, Hunstanton and other places along the Lincolnshire and Norfolk coasts.

Following the opening of the Dock the number of ships trading to Boston rapidly increased and Palmer found plenty of work. His business prospered so that in due course he was able to extend his fleet, although not in Boston. He bought a large house on Boston's High Street whose garden stretched down to the banks of the Witham. Preferring business to gardening he built rows of terraced houses for rent in the grounds and as a result became Boston's largest ratepayer and one of the respected worthies of the town. He never served his time at sea nor obtained a Board of Trade certificate so that the title Captain which was bestowed on him locally was an honorary one due to his business as tug owner. He died in July 1918 aged 76.

Frederick Palmer did not enjoy a monopoly with his tugs in Boston, as the Boston Steam Tug Co. had been trading since 1859 when they bought the wooden paddle tug CUMBRIAN (66/1859). In 1875 she was replaced by BOSTON (69/1875) which served them until 1902 when they sold her to owners on the Tyne. Other tugs appeared for a while and then disappeared to other ports so whether there was sufficent work for all the tugs in the port is a matter for further research. Palmer obtained a contract at Southamton and sent the MAY FLOWER there after the 1888 summer season. He then sent her to Cork for garrison duties, serving the various military forts and establishments around the harbour.

A move to Cork

Palmer's son Frederick went with the MAY FLOWER to Cork and lived for a short period on Spike Island in Cork Harbour before moving to Ringaskiddy where he later opened a shipyard. The family had a second MAY FLOWER built in Hull in 1889 which was registered under the ownership of Mrs. Fanny Palmer. This MAY FLOWER also went to Ireland.

Most transatlantic liners called at Queenstown (now Cobh) in Cork Harbour and from here a stream of Irish emigrants headed for a new life in America. Frederick's business prospered: he obtained contracts from the War Office and the Admiralty to tow coal and water barges to the naval ships and to tow targets for gunnery practice. He also had a contract to service lightships along the south-eastern coast of Ireland.

MAY FLOWER - probably the second of the name built in 1889 - at Merchant's Quay, Cork. On board are members of the family of her master, Captain Arthur Harrison who was originally from Boston. *[G. Lewis collection]*

By 1903 his yard had acquired sufficient skill to build a wooden coastal cargo vessel, the PERSEVERANCE, but unfortunately she rotted away prematurely because the elm used to build her from a local farm had not been properly seasoned. She was of composite construction, built of wood on an iron frame.

In 1907 the MINER was purchased and soon after the ALEXANDRA came into the fleet, being fitted with a new engine at the Palmer's yard at Ringaskiddy. By this time Frederick's three sons had entered the business, Samuel, Ralph and Richard Frederick and they traded as S.R. and R.F. Palmer. In 1913 they acquired the trawler SHARK from the Boston Fisheries and Ice Co. Ltd. (later to be known as the Boston Deep Sea Fisheries). This useful vessel performed a variety of jobs including towing, salvage and anchor retrieval.

Frederick Palmer senior, who remained in Boston, financed the additional vessels for the Cork fleet. Correspondence between his sons, grandsons and him referred to cheques from customers which were forwarded to Frederick, and on more than one occasion he was asked to advance money for certain projects at Cork. On 26th April 1911 the four-masted barque FALLS OF GARRY (2,026/1886) drove on to the Quay Rock off Ballymacus Point in thick fog and was badly holed. She was on a voyage from Australia to Glasgow with a cargo of wheat. In a letter dated 29th April 1911 Ralph Palmer advised his grandfather that he had been to the wreck with Mr. Ensor with a view to attempting to refloat her. The

SHARK tows the four-masted barque ARCHIBALD RUSSELL (2,385/1905) up the River Lee to Cork in September 1938. The bow of the MORSECOCK can just be seen alongside the barque, and a Kelly collier is at the quay. [Cork Examiner]

wreck was to be auctioned the following week and Ralph wished to know if his grandfather would advance the cash needed for working expenses. As it turned out, the barque was too badly damaged to be worth salving. After her master, Captain Roberts, and the six remaining members of her crew had been taken off by rocket apparatus she was left for the sea to break up.

The small town of Cobh was the base of the renowned salvage firm Thomas Ensor & Son who undertook a number of notable operations using their own small vessels including ADELAIDE (70/1876) and LYONESSE (382/1889). But some of the more complex jobs required additional vessels and Ensors frequently chartered the SHARK. In 1915 she assisted in salvaging the brand new bucket dredger SILURUS (1,925/1915) which, whilst waiting to be towed to Bombay, had broken her moorings on the Gareloch in the Clyde and drifted ashore. As the tide receded she capsized with her funnel and bucket frame sinking deep into the mud. Ensor righted the dredger which was ultimately delivered to India.

SHARK saw further service on the Clyde in 1923 and 1924 when Ensor was involved in the aftermath of a collision between the outward bound Canadian Pacific liner METAGAMA (12,420/1914) and the inward bound BARON VERNON (2,603/1922) which sank on an even keel in the deep water channel close to Dumbarton Rock. The death of Thomas Ensor's son Henry in 1927 along with the fact that the company had got deeply in debt due to the length of

time required to raise the BARON VERNON caused the salvage firm to close.

The MORSECOCK

In 1921 Palmers purchased the well-known ocean-going tug STORMCOCK from the Admiralty and renamed her MORSECOCK. The STORMCOCK had been built for William Hill's Liverpool Screw Towing and Lighterage Co. who chartered her to the Government for service in Alexandria in 1881 and in the following year sold her to the Admiralty. Much of STORMCOCK's time in Admiralty ownership was spent on the Queenstown station. Following the sinking of the LUSITANIA (30,396/1907) on 7th May 1915 she was employed in the recovery of many of the bodies, 170 of which were buried in Clonmel Cemetery just outside of the town.

In early March 1925 the Canadian Pacific Liner MONTLAURIER (17,000/1907) suffered damage to her steering gear in storm conditions when a thousand miles west of Fastnet and turned back to shelter in Cork Harbour. Near the narrow entrance of the Harbour she got into difficulties and ran on to a sandbank from which she was unable to extricate herself. The MORSECOCK was immediately despatched from Cobh and managed to tow the liner off the sandbank. The Dutch ocean-going tug ZWARTE ZEE (171/1917) was engaged as lead tug and with the MORSECOCK acting as stern tug the liner was successfully towed into the safety of Cork Harbour. The MONTLAURIER was unable to

MORSECOCK at anchor in Cork Harbour. *[G. Lewis collection]*

continue her voyage so the MORSECOCK and SHARK were employed in transferring her 500 passengers, baggage, mail and perishable goods to the MONTCLARE (16,314/1922) to continue the voyage to St. John, New Brunswick.

Mersey ferries

In 1927 the Palmer Brothers purchased the Mersey ferries ROSE and LILY which were renamed AN SAORSTAT (Irish for *Free State*) and FAILTE (Irish for *Welcome*) respectively. These vessels along with the MORSECOCK were employed mainly as tenders to the liners which anchored in Cork Harbour, but were also popular as excursion steamers. They were based on Dublin prior to moving to Cork Harbour.

Palmers' experience of salvage was put to good use when the coaster ZILLAH (373/1901) outward bound from Cork collided with the incoming coaster ALISON (272/1905) of Newcastle-upon-Tyne on 22nd October 1928. The ALISON was badly holed and immediately began to sink by the head. After a gallant attempt to tow her into shallow water by the Government passenger launch 199, she went down quickly. Luckily all her crew were taken off by HMS SEAWOLF.

The Palmer brothers successfully raised the ALISON by the unusual use of their passenger tenders AN SAORSTAT and FAILTE. Large beams were placed between the vessels which straddled the sunken vessel. By means of strong winches and cables the ALISON was raised in stages and beached on the foreshore where a large wooden patch was placed on the outside of her hull on the starboard side of the

well deck where the ZILLAH's bow had driven into her. The ZILLAH sustained only minor damage above the waterline which was soon repaired at Rushbrooke Dockyard, Cork.

On 10th December 1928 the White Star liner CELTIC (21,904/1901) ran on to the rocks off Roches Point at the entrance to Cork Harbour. The MORSECOCK tried to refloat her but all attempts failed and the liner was cut up where she stranded, the task lasting until 1933. During this period the MORSECOCK acted as base ship for the operation.

Frederick Palmer junior returned to Boston in 1910 and some years later as a hobby purchased the small steamer DURAS (131/1893) from the Galway Bay Steam Boat Co. Ltd., had her converted to an auxiliary motorship and operated her out of Boston. He died in 1932, the same year that his sons purchased the celebrated ROYAL IRIS from Wallasey Corporation and stationed her at Dublin until transferring her to Cork in May 1937. Details of her earlier exploits at Zeebrugge were briefly related in *Record 3*. In 1946 Palmers sold the ROYAL IRIS to the Cork Harbour Commissioners who renamed her BLARNEY.

Palmers retained their last vessel, ALEXANDRA, until September 1955 when she was delivered to a breakers yard in Dublin thus ending 70 years of tug and coastal shipowning by three generations of the family. The site of Palmers yard and workshops at Ringaskiddy is now occupied by the recently constructed Ferry Terminal. *[Palmers' fleet list and further photographs will appear in Record 7]*

The White Star's CELTIC went ashore off Roches Point on 10th December 1928. Within a few days, her funnels were cut down as they obstructed the beam from a lighthouse above and behind the photographer. MORSECOCK is alongside the CELTIC's bows. The liner remained fast and was broken up by 1933. *[Peter Thomas collection]*

AN SAORSTAT and FAILTE engaged in salvaging the ALISON which sank in the fairway between Cork and Haulbowline in 1928. The lower photograph, taken from from the upper deck of the FAILTE, shows the ALISON suspended from steel beams rigged between the two tenders. [Both: Richard Palmer collection]

WHALE SHIP CONVERSIONS
Part Two
Peter Newall

After the invention of the harpoon gun and steam catcher by Svend Foyn in 1863, the next milestone in modern whaling came with the introduction of the stern ramp in 1925. Up to that point, whales had to be stripped alongside factory ships, or at specially-built processing plants ashore. The Norwegians, having virtually eradicated whale stocks along their own coastline, were also unhappy about having to negotiate with the British for licences in the Antarctic, and wished to roam the oceans at will in search of whales. All this changed when a whale gunner, Petter Sørlle, successfully submitted two patents for stern ramps (one for single screw ships and the other for those with twin screws) which effectively overcame the design problems which had confounded ship builders, i.e. what to do about the steering mechanism, rudders and propellers. After the first stern ramp was fitted on LANCING in 1925, there was no looking back and, four years later, the first purpose-built factory ship KOSMOS arrived on the scene.

The difficulties of fitting stern ramps varied from ship to ship. The ideal was a twin screw, engines-amidships vessel like PELAGOS (ex ATHENIC) where the ramp jutted out just above the waterline before rising up to finish a short way along the stern – water ballast would be used to lower the ramp during whaling operations (top right opposite). For an engines-aft ship like the former Eagle Oil tanker SAN NAZARIO (now THORSHAMMER), however, the problems are all too clear, with a long ramp over the engine room, and running between twin funnels which have replaced the original single stack (opposite page bottom).

The photograph of THORSHAMMER in Wilton Fijenoord's yard in Rotterdam also shows the funnel marking of Thor Dahl which can still be seen today, long after the company's association with this unpleasant trade – nowadays, many seem to think that the motif is a fish, whereas it is, in fact, a whale.
[Laurence Dunn Collection]

LANCING (above)
Charles Connell & Co., Glasgow; 1898, 7,464 gt, 470 feet
LANCING had been built as the KNIGHT ERRANT for Liverpool owners Greenshields, Cowie & Co., better known as the Knight Line. The Knight ships operated mainly between Liverpool and the Far East, before the company was bought by Alfred Holt in 1917. Sold in 1914 as the RIO TIETE, she was bought by the Russian Volunteer Fleet Association and renamed OMSK the following year, and after the Russian Revolution in 1917 she was requisitioned by the British Government. Following two subsequent sales as CALANDA and FLACKWELL, she was bought by Globus Hvalfangerselkapet (Melsom & Melsom) of Larvik in 1925 and converted into a whaler. After a successful whaling career, this pioneer ship was torpedoed and sunk off Cape Hatteras in April 1942, whilst bound for New York with a cargo of oil.[Alex Duncan]

ORWELL
Charles Connell & Co., Glasgow; 1905, 7,175 gt, 470 feet
Coincidentally, in the same year as LANCING was bought by the Norwegians, another ex-Knight Line vessel, KNIGHT TEMPLAR (middle), was acquired from Alfred Holt by Tønsberg Hvalfangerei (manager Hans Borge) to become the whale oil refinery ORWELL (bottom). The second ship in the fleet with this name, the first was bought in 1911 from the Indian Steamship Co. as ORWELL and retained her original name up to her sale in 1925. The second ORWELL survived the war, and remained with her owners until her demolition at Hamburg in 1954. Photographed by Laurence Dunn at Sandefjord in 1951, prior to her southbound voyage, she had recently been modernised into a transport ship with accommodation for some 250 men.
[Laurence Dunn]

THE GRAND OLD LADY

PELAGOS

Harland & Wolff, Belfast; 1901, 12,234 gt, 500 feet

The ATHENIC (top) was the first of a new series of flush decked liners built for the Oceanic Steam Navigation Co. Ltd., better known as the White Star Line. Specifically designed for the joint White Star and Shaw Savill & Albion New Zealand service, ATHENIC and her near-identical sisters CORINTHIC and IONIC had a large refrigerated cargo capacity for frozen meat, and considerable space for almost 700 passengers in three classes.

On Valentines Day, 1902 ATHENIC set off on her maiden voyage from London to Wellington, via the Cape. Very popular with passengers, the trio brought about a change in the standing of Shaw Savill & Albion and were soon followed by further new ships. ATHENIC hit the headlines again in 1912 when farmers assisted by crew loaded their produce during a stevedore's strike in Wellington. At the outbreak of war ATHENIC was called up for service as a New Zealand troop transport and was renamed H.M.N.Z.T. No. 11. In 1916 she brought home from Santa Cruz, Tenerife, prisoners from the German raider MÖWE, which during its first cruise early that year had captured or sunk 15 merchant ships in six weeks.

After hostilities, the ships returned to their original route and, as she and her sisters were approaching the end of their intended lives, ATHENIC was purchased in 1928 by A/S Pelagos (Bruun & von der Lippe) of Tønsberg, and converted by Smiths Dock, South Bank-on-Tees into a whale factory ship. Renamed PELAGOS she emerged much altered, her elegant Harland & Wolff lines gone forever (middle).

For the next twelve years, PELAGOS operated under the Norwegian flag until January 1941 when she was captured together with the factory ships OLE WEGGER and SOLGLIMT, plus 11 catchers, by the German auxiliary cruiser PINGUIN (ex Hansa KANDELFELS). With all these ships seized within a day, this was the largest prize haul in the shortest time by a raider. Used by the Germans as a U-boat depot ship in Norwegian waters, she was later returned to her owners in 1945 and rebuilt with an extended superstructure (bottom and opposite page top), and was finally broken up at Hamburg in June 1962. *[Top and middle: Peter Newall Collection; bottom: Alex Duncan; opposite page top: Laurence Dunn]*

MORE RUNICS

Since the publication of part one of this feature, two unusual photographs of the White Star vessels RUNIC have emerged. The first shows the 1889 RUNIC as the whale oil ship IMO (middle) after her collision with MONT BLANC which resulted in the largest man-made explosion prior to Hiroshima, and immense loss of life at Halifax, Nova Scotia on 6th December 1917. The MONT BLANC was blown to smithereens whilst the IMO was later successfully salvaged. Note the lettering on her side – Belgian Relief! *[Paul Louden-Brown Collection]*

The second RUNIC is shown below immediately after her rebuild as NEW SEVILLA in 1930. Compare this with the state of the ship shown on page 46 of *Record 5*. It is also interesting to note that, after conversion, she managed to maintain some of her former looks, unlike PELAGOS. *[Salvesen Collection, University of Edinburgh]*

SOUTH GEORGIA

Since their discovery in 1675, the remote islands of South Georgia were of little interest to the British or any other nation, that is until the arrival of C. A. Larsen and the first whaling ships at Grytviken in 1904. The British, recognising the commercial opportunities of this long-forgotten territory, soon claimed sovereignty over South Georgia and it became a dependency of the Falkland Islands. As word spread of the large stocks of whales in the area, more and more Norwegian companies applied for concessions for whaling stations at South Georgia and neighbouring islands and, by 1914, 24 licenses were granted, and buildings sprang up everywhere. The conditions ashore were not much better than on the ships with a foul smell everywhere, and made worse by the extreme cold. Even in 1950, a visiting surgeon described South Georgia as 'the most sordid, unsanitary habitation of white men to be found the world over, and the most nauseating example of what commercial greed can do at the expense of human dignity.'

CORONDA (opposite page, upper)
William Gray & Co., West Hartlepool; 1892, 2,733 gt, 310 feet
Christian Salvesen of Leith was one of the few British companies to have a base in South Georgia. The aptly named Leith Harbour was established in 1909 and, early the following year, CORONDA carried the first cargo of whale oil back to Scotland. Built as MANICA in 1892, this vessel was one of nine new steamers built for the British & Colonial Steam Navigation Co. Ltd. (Bucknall Brothers) to serve a major contract the company had won in South Africa for the transportation of material from Amsterdam for the new Netherlands South Africa Railway which linked the land-locked Transvaal Republic with Delagoa Bay (Lourenço Marques) in Moçambique. Sporting the 'Bucknall's teeth' funnel markings, all the new ships had shallow drafts so that they could negotiate the bars at East London and Durban. Transferred to Bucknall Nephews in 1899 and renamed CORONDA, she was sold to Salvesens in 1908, her name unchanged. Her end came in 1917 when she was torpedoed by U 81 180 miles north west of Tory Island whilst on a voyage to South Georgia. The loss of nine lives probably prompted the company to repeat her name in a second CORONDA in 1922 – see page 44 of *Record 5.*
[Salvesen Collection, University of Edinburgh]

In addition to all the other hazards, fire was always a potential problem for the ships – in 1916 HORATIO (see page 36 of *Record 5*) suffered a catastrophic fire in Leith Harbour when her cargo of 2,000 tons of whale oil caught alight (opposite page bottom).
[Salvesen Collection, University of Edinburgh]

THE SHIP WHICH REFUSES TO DIE

BRUTUS
J. Reid & Co., Glasgow; 1883, 1,620 gt, 249 feet
In Prince Olav Harbour lies one the most astonishing survivors of the whaling era. Built as the three-masted steel sailing ship SIERRA PEDROSA for the Sierra Shipping Co. of Liverpool, she was one of a large well-maintained fleet of white ships, all bearing the SIERRA prefix, and trading mainly to Rangoon. In August 1889 with a cargo of coal, she stranded on Woodstock beach, Cape Town during one of the infamous Cape north west gales (this page, upper). On that occasion she was refloated, but when, thirteen years later almost to the day, she went aground in the same spot, as the newly named BRUTUS, she was not so lucky. This time she was severely damaged and was later salvaged to become a cold store hulk in Table Bay. In 1917 she was bought by Southern Whaling & Sealing, which at that time was managed by Irvin & Johnson, a local Cape Town fishing firm. In February 1918 she arrived at their South Georgia base Prince Olav Harbour, towed by the catchers TRULS and TRAVELLER. Until the closure of the station in 1931, she served as a coal hulk. This remarkable view of BRUTUS was taken in 1987 by George Mortimore who was Chief Officer of the RFA SIR LANCELOT which can be seen in the background (this page bottom).
[Cape Archives E8658 and George Mortimore]

EAGLE OIL CONVERSIONS

Shortly after the formation of the Eagle Oil Transport Co. in 1912, the company ordered a series of ships which were the super tankers of their day. In the 1920s five of these SAN ships were sold on to become whale factory ships – C.A.LARSEN (SAN GREGORIO), OLE WEGGER (SAN LORENZO), THORSHAMMER (SAN NAZARIO), SOUTHERN EMPRESS (SAN JERONIMO), and SOUTHERN PRINCESS (SAN PATRICIO). The first two were built at Swan Hunter and were featured in Swans and Eagles – *Record 4*.

Of the five, probably the most interesting was C.A.LARSEN because she was the only whale factory ship to have a bow door. This was fitted mainly because of the problems with stern ramps fitted to engines-aft ships, and also as a way of getting round Petter Sørlle's patent. In the end, the conversion was very expensive and although the door worked well, the problems closing it whilst underway persuaded most owners that the stern ramp was the best solution.

The bow doors are clearly visible in the upper view showing C.A.LARSEN in the Port Chalmers Dry Dock after her 1928 grounding in New Zealand. In 1946, she had another adventure when, as the ANTARCTIC (lower photograph), her rudder and propeller sustained serious damage in the ice. She was towed by PELAGOS more than 3,000 miles from the Antarctic to Cape Town, probably one of the longest and most hazardous tows ever undertaken – the average speed was around four knots whilst the longest days run was 128 miles, and the shortest, minus 50 miles! *[Ian J. Farquhar Collection]*

As a contrast to the C.A. LARSEN, the SOUTHERN PRINCESS owned by Southern Whaling & Sealing is shown with her stern ramp. Built in 1915 as SAN PATRICIO, she was converted into a whaler in 1929. Purchased by Salvesens in 1940, she was torpedoed whilst on a voyage from North America to Britain in 1943 with the loss of four lives. *[Peter Newall Collection]*

MORE TANKERS

THORØY
Armstrong, Mitchell and Co. Ltd., Newcastle-upon-Tyne; 1893, 2,710gt, 294 feet
Thor Dahl owned an old Armstrong, Mitchell tanker which had been built for C.T.Bowring & Co. Ltd., Liverpool as SNOWFLAKE. In 1913 she was sold to an Antwerp company and renamed KREMLIN. Requisitioned for the war years as a Royal Fleet Auxiliary, she returned to her owner in 1918. Purchased in 1922 by the Hvalfanger A/S Vestfold (J. Rasmussen & Co.), Sandefjord she was VELLØY for two years until her sale to Bryde & Dahls as THORØY, a name she kept until 1947. Her final years prior to demolition in 1953 were spent as the Turkish tanker ANNE DE FRANCE. *[Alex Duncan]*

ANGLO NORSE

Palmers Shipbuilding & Iron Co. Ltd., Newcastle-upon-Tyne; 1914, 6,960 gt, 425 feet

This ugly ship represents the nadir or zenith of whaling, depending on your perspective. The top photograph shows her entering Todd's Brooklyn shipyard in 1949 for what is described as a 27-hour clean up after a seven-month whale hunt in the South Pacific during which time 2,500 sperm whales were slaughtered, yielding oil valued at $4 million. Seeking whales in some of the most sensitive spots of the globe including Madagascar, Chile and Australia, the ANGLO NORSE operated under different flags and registrations when convenient to legitimise her operation. The worst instance of this was in the early 1950s when she hunted in French territorial waters under the French flag owned by a company whose formation had been assisted by the whaling magnate Anders Jahre.

Built as the tanker MARICOPA for Wilhelm Wilhelmsen, she was sold in 1929 to the jointly owned Norwegian and British company Falkland Shipowners Ltd. of London. Converted into a whale oil refinery at the Götaverken shipyard, Göteborg, she was renamed ANGLO NORSE. Purchased by the Ministry of War Transport in 1941, she was seriously damaged in a fire and scuttled later that year. After repairs, she emerged as the EMPIRE NORSE (middle) and, in 1946, returned to her pre-war owners. In 1957, as the JANINA, she suffered another conflagration and sank north west of Oporto. *[Top: Laurence Dunn collection; middle and bottom: Ian J. Farquhar collection]*

The final part of this article in *Record 7* will feature, amongst others, some liners and cable ships which were converted to whale ships.

CONNELL BROTHERS LTD
David Burrell

Charles Connell (1822-1884), from Ayrshire, was apprenticed to Robert Steele and Company. He went on to become yard manager at Alex Stephen and Sons for some five years before commencing shipbuilding on his own account in 1861 at Scotstoun, as Charles Connell and Company (Ltd. from 1902). Despite the yard being idle from 1931 to 1937, over 500 ships were delivered before, in 1968, the yard became the Scotstoun Division of Upper Clyde Shipbuilders in the aftermath of the Geddes Report. It closed in 1980.

When he died in February 1884 Charles Connell left a widow, seven sons and three daughters. Like many shipbuilders the family branched out into owning, which gave employment for his fifth son Arthur and provided work for the yard, especially when orders were scarce.

In November 1900 Napier and Connell Ltd. was established by John Napier and Arthur Connell. Half the authorised capital of £100,000 was issued to finance the first ship, £25,000 to members of the Connell family and £25,000 to the Napiers and McIntyre (Glasgow iron merchants). The Connell shares were taken up by four of the brothers, Charles (1854-1913), William (1864-1934), John (1869-1937) and Arthur (1872-1949). On 11th October 1901 Scotstoun launched KILBRIDE, a typical three island tramp and sister to the earlier ORONSAY (3,761/1900), DUNBAR (3,672/1900) and KINCRAIG (3,707/1901). Her price was £48,000.

Napier and Connell Ltd
Connell Brothers Ltd
Company Number: 4661
Incorporated: 3.11.1900
Renamed: 9.11.1907
Voluntary liquidation: 11.2.1920
Capital:
£100,000 (£100 shares). 26.4.1907 reduced to £50,000 (£50 shares), shareholders receiving £50 cash per share.
500 shares distributed 2.1901, another 250 in 12.1903 and the remaining 250 in 5.1908.
Directors (*managing):

C.B. Connell	1900-13, died 23.5.1913	
A.C. Connell*	1900-20	
J. McIntyre	1900-05, died 7.11.1905	
J. Napier*	1900-07, resigned 5.1907	
W.C.S. Connell	1907-20	
J.C. Connell	1909-20	

Funnel: red with black top
Houseflag: divided vertically red and blue with white diamond

---

Thomas Smith, born in Liverpool in 1867, was appointed master of KILBRIDE. This was his first regular command after brief spells as master since passing for his ticket in 1892. In 1906 he transferred

to KILKERRAN. Leaving Connells in 1909 he died in 1934 whilst master of GRETASTON (5,008/1924).

The principal trade for Napier and Connell was to the East Indies, including India and Burma. The freight market had peaked in 1900, buoyed by demands for shipping from the Spanish American War, Boer War and Boxer Rising, and was now causing concern as it slipped back. On completion in November 1901 KILBRIDE loaded at Liverpool for Calcutta. Her eleven month maiden voyage was:
Liverpool (sailed 18.11.01) - Calcutta (arrived 30.12.01/sailed 22.1.02) - Rangoon (28.1/20.2) - Bombay (5.3/20.3) - Kobe (18.4/26.4) - Kuchinotzu - Singapore (16.5/25.5) - Sourabaya - Philadelphia (5.8/21.8) - Fernandina (——/28.8) - Hamburg (8.10).

As with all tramp fleets coal was a regular outward cargo, often loaded in Welsh ports for the Plate, East Indies and elsewhere. A snap view of the fleet in May 1906 gives the picture:

Fleet position - 24th May 1906
KILBRIDE
    Bombay sailed May 6 Calcutta arrived May 15
KILBRENNAN
    Barry sailed May 3   for Diego Suarez
KILCHATTAN
    Calcutta sailed Apr 12 Bombay arrived April 23
KILKERRAN
    Saleef   Calcutta arrived April 25
Source:Lloyd's Weekly Shipping Index

As the shipbuilding market weakened an order was placed for a sister to KILBRIDE, launched in March 1903 as KILBRENNAN. The shortage of work and state of the shipping market was reflected in her price, £37,000. She was part financed by distributing £25,000 of the unissued shares. The outbreak of war between Russia and Japan in 1904 had little effect on the market as the increased demands from the belligerents, such as the chartering of scores of colliers to fuel the Russian Baltic fleet on its passage east to annihilation at the Battle of Tsushima, were offset by depressed trade elsewhere.

KILBRENNAN was to be the only marine loss in the fleet when, on 28th March 1907, she struck an uncharted obstruction three miles off Riet Point, East of Port Alfred, near East London. A Court of Inquiry held at Port Elizabeth on 15-16th April attached no blame to her master, James Wilson. She was being navigated in a proper and seamanlike manner, on a safe course in clear weather when she struck. Headed for the shore she settled so fast that 25 minutes later she sank 2.5 miles offshore outside the edge of the breakers, in 10½ fathoms. Four of the crew drowned when they went to the forecastle for their clothes, against orders.

Owners often dispensed with the services of a master who lost his ship, whether or not he was to blame. Wilson (1863-1919) from Port Glasgow, whose first command had been the steel barque ARETHUSA (1,279/1891) in 1897, was more fortunate; he was given KILLIN new in 1908 and retained her until sunk by EMDEN. He then took LOYALTY, ex EMPRESS OF INDIA (5,934/1891), and died as her master in March 1919. Purchased from Canadian Pacific and refitted as a hospital ship, she was the contribution of the Maharaja of Gwalior to the Allied war effort.

Early in 1906 KILCHATTAN and KILKERRAN were commissioned, spar deckers as opposed to the two-deck design of the earlier ships. They cost £39,150 each. The change from full scantlings to spar decks was probably made in the light of the trading pattern of the fleet. KILKERRAN's maiden voyage was typical of the period for the fleet:
Clyde (sailed 12.2.1906) - Cardiff (arrived 14.2/sailed 23.2) - Aden (16.3/23.3) - Saleef - Calcutta (25.4/3.6) - Kurrachee (17.6/12.7) - Belfast (17.8).

The year 1907 was an eventful one. KILBRENNAN was lost in March, the Connells bought out the Napier and McIntyre shareholdings in May, and John Napier resigned as a managing director. Two of the younger Connell brothers, Alfred and Allan, each received a nominal share. The share capital had been halved in March, payment of £50 in cash being made on each £100 share. This would indicate that the company had been performing well, both commissioning new ships and accumulating funds for distribution. The insurance settlement for KILBRENNAN undoubtedly helped. The reason for the buyout is not now known. It may have resulted from disagreement on policy, or the deaths of James Napier and John McIntyre (in January and November

1905) and incompatibility of the survivors. James Glen resigned as company secretary at the same time, and the company was restyled Connell Brothers Ltd. in November 1907.

John Napier and James Glen went on to found the Gleneden Steamship Co. Ltd. in 1909, and successfully operated the ship of that name (4,735/1909) until she was wrecked off Anglesey in January 1940. The company was then wound up and £78,000 was distributed to the holders of the £20,000 capital.

The last addition to the fleet entered service in April 1908. KILLIN was another spar decker, slightly smaller than the earlier ships. Costing £42,211, she was in part financed by issuing the balance of the authorised capital, 250 £50 shares. The shareholdings of Alfred and Allan benefited, as each received forty shares to add to the single ones received the previous year.

In May 1910 John Eno, from South Shields, took command of KILCHATTAN. He was transferred to KILKERRAN in 1913 and remained with her until shortly before the fleet was sold. His first command had been SPECIALIST (2,844/1890) in 1904, whilst in October 1906 he had lost the Horsley Line's SERBURY (3,873/1905). Some masters are not as fortunate as others, and both KILCHATTAN and KILKERRAN went ashore under his command (February 1911 in the Gulf of Suez and September 1914 near Rangoon), but got off without assistance or damage. Remaining at sea until 1935 his last command was Lawther, Latta's ANGLO-PERUVIAN (5,457/1926) from 1926.

After a decade of poor returns the freight market boomed in the 'Golden Year' of 1911. Sadly, Charles Connell died in May 1913. Having been ill for some time past he failed to recover from an operation a few days earlier. The summer of 1911 also saw David

The Connell and Napier partnership broke up in 1907, John Napier and James Glen subsequently forming the Gleneden Steamship Co. Ltd. Its steamer GLENEDEN was built by Scotts of Greenock in 1909 and survived until 1940 when wrecked after almost completing a voyage from Saigon to Liverpool with a cargo of rice.
[George Scott collection]

Wilson from Fife take command of KILKERRAN. Moving to KILBRIDE in 1913 he joined the Bay Steamship Company when they purchased her. The fleet was fully employed, the position of the ships at the end of May 1912 being:

The Balkan Wars erupted in 1912 and caused disruption in the Black Sea trades when Turkey closed the Dardanelles to traffic. Thereafter rates dropped off until war in 1914, at which point the industry was paralysed, some owners delaying sailings from British ports in view of the perceived war risk. The War Risk P&I Clubs and the Government rapidly organised cover and soon the ships were back at sea.

On 4th August 1914 Britain went to war. The assassination of Archduke Franz Ferdinand, heir to the Austrian throne, at Sarajevo on 28th June echoed through the corridors of power as treaties drew country after country into the maelstrom of the First World War. Ernest Hemingway (1899-1961) later termed it '... the most colossal, murderous, mismanaged butchery that has ever taken place...'

The ships were all away from home, KILBRIDE at Montevideo and the other three scattered between Aden and Calcutta. KILLIN sailed east from Aden and loaded 6,000 tons of coal at Calcutta for Colombo. Proceeding down the Hughli, Captain Wilson was unaware that the German cruiser EMDEN was off the Heads sinking shipping until, in the early hours of 13th September, she was sighted. There was no hope of escape from her 24 knots and ten 10.5cm guns. The crew were transferred to the captured KABINGA (4,657/1907) and KILLIN was sunk. The next day KABINGA and all on board were released. The receipt of £32,000 from war risk insurance was little consolation for the loss of the youngest ship in the fleet.

EMDEN had been detached from the China Squadron as a commerce raider. She sank sixteen merchant ships, the Russian cruiser ZHEMTCHUG and the French destroyer MOUSQUET. Madras was shelled, next was the Cocos Island cable station. But the first ANZAC troop convoy to Europe was passing 50 miles to the south with a heavy escort. Sighting EMDEN the cable staff broadcast an unknown ship warning. Heard by the convoy, HMAS SYDNEY was detached to investigate. Faster and better gunned than EMDEN, there was no escape and the rusting remains of EMDEN lay on North Keeling reef until broken up by Japanese salvors in 1950. Only EMDEN's landing party escaped to reach Constantinople in May 1915.

The days of the Connell fleet were now numbered; within eighteen months it would be no more. Not only had KILLIN been sunk, but Major Alfred Connell was killed in France on 28th September 1915. At the time commanding officer of the 2nd Royal Scots Fusiliers he fell in the German counter-attacks following the Battle of Loos. The remaining ships were sold and, like KILLIN, were all lost before peace returned in November 1918. The company itself survived a little longer, being placed in voluntary liquidation in February 1920. So ended this venture into shipowning, although the family were to return to the arena again in the 1950s and 1960s.

Arthur Connell returned to shipbuilding, being chairman of Charles Connell and Company Ltd from 1937 until his death in 1949. He, like his brothers, was a noted yachtsman owning, amongst others, ORONSEY and WESTRA. His brother, John Connell, had owned ZINITA.

The war in Europe settled down to a slogging match in the mud, with the hope of an early victory and 'Home for Christmas' unfulfilled. KILBRIDE continued about her business, proceeding from Montevideo to Batavia and Liverpool. Then another Plate trip before being taken up as Collier 729 on 22nd May 1915. She remained requisitioned until lost in March 1916. KILKERRAN became Collier 694 on 1st June 1915. At Calcutta when war was declared she loaded at Rangoon for Liverpool, and made another trip (Cardiff to Aden, Calcutta, Rangoon and Liverpool) before being requisitioned and loading coal at Cardiff for Halifax. Service as an Expeditionary Force Transport to France followed before release on 4th November 1915.

The reasons which saw the sale of the fleet are now unknown. Danger from enemy action, which had seen KILLIN sunk (fortunately no lives were lost with any of the three ships sunk by the enemy, and only one was injured), the death of Alfred Connell and rising ship values probably all played their part and led, in December 1915, to agreement to sell the three remaining ships to the Bay Steamship Company Ltd. The prices realised reflected the wartime market. KILBRIDE, under requisition, fetched £65,000 and the two others £90,000 each. Proceeds of £245,000 compared to the newbuilding cost of £126,300 for the three resulted in a profit of £118,700. The transaction was brokered by Furness,

Withy and Co. Ltd., in whose name the ships were registered for a few days when transferred in February/March 1916.

As a wartime exigency the British Government refused to allow the transfer of ships abroad, so the French Government formed the British-flag Bay Steamship Co. Ltd., with the assistance of the Hudson's Bay Company, to buy tonnage to meet French needs. KILBRIDE, taken over on 5th February, was sunk before she could be renamed, but would likely have become BAYBRIDE. The others became BAYCHATTAN and BAYKERRAN.

BAYCHATTAN was torpedoed by UC 50 off Prawle Point in October 1917, her war risk insurance payment being £39,000. This left BAYKERRAN, until January 1918 when she reported by wireless telegraphy that she was disabled in heavy North Atlantic weather. Then nothing: she had foundered, taking with her Captain Reid and all her crew. She was posted missing at Lloyd's on 3rd April. An American cruiser searched the area but found no trace of either ship or crew.

Shareholdings:					
Date	2.1901	12.1903	5.1907	5.1908	
Charles Broadfoot Connell	50	75	150	190	died 23.5.13
William Cuthbert Smith Connell	50	75	147	187	
John Campbell Connell	50	75	150	190	
James Napier	50	75	—-	—-	died 1.1.05
Arthur Cuthbert Connell	100	150	300	350	
John McIntyre	50	75	—-	—-	died 7.11.05
John Napier	100	150	—-	—-	
George G. Napier	50	75	—-	—-	
Margaret Ann Ferguson or Connell	—-	—-	1	1	
Alfred Hamilton Connell	—-	—-	1	41	killed 28.9.15
Allan Macgregor Connell	—-	—-	1	41	

Fleet list

1. **KILBRIDE** 1901-1916
O.N. 113986 3,712g 2,385n 6,050d 354.1 x 45.0 x 25.8 feet
T. 3-cyl. by Dunsmuir & Jackson Ltd, Glasgow; bores 25, 41 & 66 ins, stroke 45 ins; 2 boilers, 170 psi; 1600 IHP, 11 knots.
11.10.1901: Launched by Charles Connell & Co., Glasgow (Yard No. 263) for Napier & Connell Ltd., Glasgow as KILBRIDE.
11.1901: Completed.
1907: Owners became Connell Brothers Ltd., Glasgow.
1916: Sold to Furness, Withy & Co. Ltd., Liverpool.
1916: Sold to the Bay Steamship Co. Ltd. (Sale & Co., managers), London.
1.3.1916: Sunk by gunfire from the German submarine U 38 thirty miles east of Galita Island, Tunis whilst on a voyage from Barry to Malta and Salonika with a cargo of coal. One member of the crew was injured.

2. **KILBRENNAN** 1903-1907
O.N. 115758 3,640g 2,332n 6,000d 353.0 x 45.0 x 25.9 feet.
T-3 cyl. by Dunsmuir & Jackson Ltd, Glasgow; bores 25, 41 & 66 ins, stroke 45 ins; 2 boilers, 170 psi;1600 IHP, 11 knots.
31.3.1903: Launched by Charles Connell & Co., Glasgow (Yard No. 276) for Napier & Connell Ltd, Glasgow as KILBRENNAN.
4.1903: Completed.
28.3.1907: Wrecked on Fish Point, East London whilst on a voyage from Barry to Diego Suarez with a cargo of coal.

3. **KILCHATTAN** 1906-1916
O.N. 121285   3,758g 2,418n 6,434d   361.8 x 47.6 x 17.9/26.5 feet. Spar deck.
T. 3-cyl. by Dunsmuir & Jackson Ltd, Glasgow; bores 25.5, 42 & 68 ins, stroke 45ins; 2 boilers, 180 psi, 1800 IHP, 10.5 knots.
13.12.1905: Launched by Charles Connell & Co, Glasgow (Yard No. 301) for Napier & Connell Ltd, Glasgow as KILCHATTAN.
1.1906: Completed.
1907: Owners became Connell Brothers Ltd., Glasgow.
1916: Sold to Furness, Withy & Co. Ltd., Liverpool.
1916: Sold to the Bay Steamship Co. Ltd. (Sale & Co., managers), London and renamed BAYCHATTAN.
11.10.1917: Torpedoed and sunk by the German submarine UC 50 half a mile south south west of Prawle Point whilst on a voyage from Havre to Cardiff in ballast.

4. **KILKERRAN** 1906-1916
O.N. 121295   3,755g 2,413n 6,434d   361.8 x 47.6 x 17.9/26.5 feet. Spar deck.
T. 3-cyl. by Dunsmuir & Jackson Ltd, Glasgow; bores 25.5, 42 & 68 ins, stroke 45ins; 2 boilers, 180 psi; 1,800 IHP, 10 knots.
23.1.1906: Launched by Charles Connell & Co., Glasgow (Yard No. 302) for Napier & Connell Ltd., Glasgow as KILKERRAN.
2.1906: Completed.
1907: Owners became Connell Brothers Ltd., Glasgow.
1916: Sold to Furness, Withy & Co. Ltd., Liverpool.
1916: Sold to the Bay Steamship Co. Ltd. (Sale & Co., managers), London and renamed BAYKERRAN.
19.1.1918: Sailed from New York for St. Nazaire with a cargo of 5,652 tons of grain and a crew of 41.
23.1.1918: Wireless telegraphy reported her disabled in position 41.14 north by 54.10 west but not since heard of.
3.4.1918: Posted missing at Lloyd's.

5. **KILLIN** 1908-1914
O.N. 124270 3,544g 2,257n 6,070d 350.0 x 46.2 x 25.8 feet. Spar deck.
T. 3-cyl. by Dunsmuir & Jackson Ltd, Glasgow; bores 25, 41 & 66 ins, stroke 45 ins; 2 boilers, 180 psi; 1800,IHP, 10.5 knots.
3.4.1908: Launched by Charles Connell & Co., Glasgow (Yard No. 318) for Connell Brothers Ltd, Glasgow as KILLIN.
4. 1908: Completed.
3.9.1914: Captured by the German cruiser SMS EMDEN and sunk by gunfire in position 17.2 north by 86.10 east whilst on a voyage from Calcutta to Colombo with a cargo of coal.

KILCHATTAN as BAYCHATTAN at Boston 25th November 1916. *[R. Hildebrand, collection of E.N. Taylor]*

KILKERRAN (above), possibly in Antwerp
[K. O'Donoghue collection]

A trials view of KILLIN (below)
[University of Glasgow Archives DC101/1273]

EVERY PICTURE TELLS A STORY

This occasional column features photographs which tell a story about the ships involved, be it concerning a casualty, a conversion, a cargo or other circumstance. Readers are welcome to submit unusual photographs.

Being aground can be a life-threatening event or an every day occurrence, depending on the ship, the circumstances, and the trade. In the case of the little steamer DARDARE, all seems routine and peaceful. She lies off Bude's Chapel Rock with at least five ropes out and a ladder over her side which almost reaches the mud she is resting on. Her upright stance shows how little steamers were designed to take the ground, and trading round the south west she would do so many times.

DARDARE was owned by William Rouse of Angle, and it is reasonable to assume she is waiting to lock into Bude to unload a cargo of coal or perhaps Pembrokeshire limestone for local limekilns. Her diminutive size is apparent from the five figures on deck and on the bridge (her entire crew, perhaps), and at 83 feet and 87 tons gross she was one of the smallest steamers running on the British coast.

DARDARE had been built of iron in Havre back in 1872, and was one of very few French-built coastal steamers to come into British ownership, which she did in September 1902. By then there seemed no recollection of who had built her hull or engines, and they were both recorded as 'unknown' in her registration documents. Her first British owner was Oliver Piper, manager of the Channel Dry Docks, Shipbuilding and Engineering Company of Passage West, Cork. Piper sold her very quickly, suggesting he had bought her as a speculation or perhaps for repair and resale. After being owned briefly in Argyllshire, Gateshead and Glasgow, DARDARE passed to William Rouse in 1904 and stayed with him until sold to a flat owner in Liverpool in 1911. Her final owner was the Grain Elevating and Automatic Weighing Co. Ltd. who would have used her around the Mersey, perhaps as a lighter as by the time her iron hull was broken up in 1925 her engines would have been over half a century old. *[Grahame Farr/Robin Craig collection]*

LANCING: THE STEAMER THAT BECAME
ONE OF THE FASTEST SAILERS
Charles Dawson

It may appear strange that a steamer which had her engines removed and began trading under sail alone would, in her new guise, actually be able to reach speeds greater than she did previously. It was certainly true of the sailing ship LANCING, Clyde-built in the 1860s as the French steamer PÉREIRE and converted after some 14 years on the transatlantic passenger run to a four-masted square-rigger sailing the great oceans of the world. How could an ex-steamer sail so well? There has been some speculation regarding the effects of such a conversion. Basil Lubbock pointed to the change in shape of a ship's stern with the propeller void filled in. Perhaps a simple explanation is the somewhat higher length/breadth ratio of steamships at the particular period when such conversions were being carried out.

Her owners, the French Compagnie Générale Transatlantique (CGT), named her PÉREIRE in honour of their founder, reflecting the prestige that was hoped for in the fight for supremacy in the important transatlantic passenger, freight and mail service. The immediate targets were to beat the crossing times of the Cunard liners, including SCOTIA, their last fling in paddle propulsion, and also the American packet ship, the wooden paddler VANDERBILT.

France at that time had little experience in the building of large iron vessels, or of their engines, so it was almost inevitable that the order should be placed in Scotland, the premier shipbuilding country of Europe at that time. She was designed by Sir William Pearce and built by the pioneering Robert Napier & Son of Govan on the River Clyde. PÉREIRE was launched there on 4th November 1865, the ceremony being performed by the wife of John, one of the two sons in the business. She was an iron screw steamer, 371 x 43.8 x 38.7 feet, 3,012 gross register tons, with three-masted barque rig, complete with clipper bow and figurehead, naturally enough of CGT's founder. She was fitted with engines with 2 x 45 inch and 2 x 84 inch diameter cylinders and 48 inch stroke. Her original four-bladed Griffiths screw was designed to give her a speed of 14.5 knots.

PÉREIRE arrived in France in 1866 and on her trials outside Cherbourg she showed promise of matching all expectations when she reached a speed of 15.3 knots. Reflecting the air of confidence, great festivities were held prior to her departure at the end of the month. She took 9 days 4 hours for her maiden crossing from Le Havre to New York, a day slower than SCOTIA. She never did quite match up to her top-notch rivals, but she was not lacking in sturdiness

The Compagnie Générale Transatlantique steamer PÉREIRE before being converted to the sailing ship LANCING.

as she showed in 1869 when she weathered a tremendous storm four days away from her home port of Brest. In 1872-3, a third pair of cylinders was added to her engine by her builders, such being a normal compounding procedure at the time as a fuel improvement measure. At the same time a second funnel was added and her original propeller was replaced by a four-bladed one of Hirsch type.

Steam to sail

In 1881 when she was in Goletta harbour, Tunis, fire broke out in her and she was temporarily sunk by torpedo to avoid endangering nearby vessels. She was soon raised, refurbished and put back into service, but at the end of 1887, after grounding near St Nazaire, her owners decided to part with her and she was sold as is to A.E. Kinnear & Co. of London. Her machinery was taken out and after a long and exacting salvage operation in the summer of 1888 she was towed to Blyth Dockyard Co. Ltd. in north east England for conversion. It was said to have nearly ruined the company.

On 5th February 1889 she left Blyth, majestically transformed into the four-masted ship LANCING, named after the Sussex village. She was fitted with three new masts and bowsprit, while the old foremast became her mizzen. Her new masts, like the great Forth Bridge just being completed, were in the up-and-coming constructional material, steel. For her sails, LANCING required three miles of yard-wide canvas. Her sharp lines and slenderness were especially noticeable in dry dock. One criticism that the purist might make was her unduly short bowsprit, sufficient to take only two jibs. Now after 22 years as a steamer, she was ready to set out on her new career that was to last nearly twice as long again and was eventually to bring her renown among a new band of admirers, the lovers of the big windjammers.

Her water-ballast tanks, still rather unusual at that time for a sailing ship, were of great value from the point of view of both economy and safety; especially in port, time could be saved because there was no need to manhandle ballast.

On her first voyage as a sailing ship, LANCING left London for Australia on 5th March 1889 with a cargo of 1,800 tons of cement, arriving in Melbourne in 108 days, about average for the big grain windjammers of later years. Her captain, George Alfred Hatfield, a real Blue-Nose skipper who had supervised her conversion, had, together with other Canadian and

Two views of PÉREIRE; the upper possibly in a US port. *[Top: John Naylon collection; bottom: National Maritime Museum P15877]*

English backers, a financial interest in her, and Mrs Hatfield had a hand in planning the interior decoration of the cabins. Even the petty officers' quarters were said to be luxurious. For the next four or so years she worked the jute route between India and Dundee with the odd call at New York. None of her passages were noteworthy, so that profits were small and she was consequently laid up in Liverpool for a time, her fate hanging in the balance.

British to Norwegian

She was bought in 1893 by Johan Bryde of Sandefjord in Norway. Although she still had some Canadian backing, she sailed for the Bryde company under the Norwegian flag, her first voyage under their ownership being from Barry to Batavia, which she reached in 90 days, a reasonable start to her new career. On the way to Calcutta, fever broke out on board and two sailors died and were buried at sea. After three years she was bought by Frank Ross of Quebec and reverted to the red ensign. At the end of 1896 she was chartered for a couple of months by an American syndicate searching for Aztec treasure in Peru. If they found anything, they did not divulge details.

From 1895 to 1901 LANCING was sailing regularly, either under the red ensign or Norwegian flag, on the trans-Pacific route, and her times showed remarkable consistency, averaging about 60 days between San Francisco and east Australian ports. In 1895 the Norwegian Captain A. Raastad sailed from Newcastle to San Francisco in 56 days, and two years later Captain Hatfield sailed 'Frisco to Sydney in 54 days.

The Norwegians took over completely, and for good, in 1901 when she was bought for £6,300 by J. Johansen & Co., and became their largest vessel. A strange coincidence was that their second largest vessel, the four-masted barque THEODOR, was non other than the converted ex-Cunard steamer CHINA, which was also built by Napiers and had been one of PÉREIRE's most serious transatlantic rivals. Yet another old rival, VANDERBILT, became the square rigger THREE BROTHERS. She ended her life as the Anchor Line's coal-hulk at Gibraltar, and survived to the ripe old age of 63.

With the Norwegians now fully in charge of LANCING, her final and really her greatest time had begun. Lubbock remarks, with some justification, that he could find no exceptional passages under the red ensign and that the Norwegians seemed finally to have got the hang of her. He also points out that she could not have been easy to handle with her great length and heavy yards, but the Norwegian skipper obviously learned how to exploit her in the open ocean where she was said to be able to bowl along in even a moderate breeze.

Slow coach to record breaker

From 1901 to 1914 New Caledonia became a regular port of call for the profitable bulk cargoes - up to over 3,000 tons - of nickel and chromium ores, and in 1915, saltpetre from Chile. Between 1903 and 1914

LANCING possibly at Ardrossan. *[National Maritime Museum P4282]*

LANCING had one of her most inspired and inspiring captains, Nils Bull Melsom, who served the longest unbroken period of any of her skippers. In 1904 he sailed the LANCING from St. John NB to Melbourne in 79 days, and in 1908 his 64 days from Lands End to Melbourne ranks amongst the fastest half-dozen times on this run. This was a staggering feat, since most other record holders were specially built and maintained clippers. The only other fast voyages down under were the swan songs of the big grain windjammers: in 1933-4 the two Laeisz P-Line four-masted barques PRIWALL and PADUA clocked 66 days from Hamburg to the Spencer Gulf in South Australia.

Captain Melsom's next feat was a time of 44 days from Montevideo to New Caledonia in 1911, a great inspiration for his mate Oscar Olufsen who served under him for a number of years and later, after Melsom's retirement during the First World War, became LANCING's most renowned skipper. In 1917 under Captain Olufsen she made her best day's run of 366 miles - beating CUTTY SARK's record by three miles - en route from Kristiansand in Norway to Matane on the St. Lawrence, Canada. An average of 18 knots in a watch was the maximum speed she attained during this run, beating the 15.3 knots she had clocked on her trials as a steamship.

A fine sequence of photographs of LANCING under sail in the Kattegat in 1916 *[National Maritime Museum P4283 and P4284, courtesy John Naylon]*

LANCING photographed by J. Dubas at Baltimore on 25th February 1917. *[John Naylon collection]*

Captain Olufsen's last great achievement was his record for the transatlantic crossing made in the middle of the First World War: 12 days 21 hours from Ambrose Light to Muckle Flugga from 1st to 14th February 1916. For the final stage of this crossing, the time of 6 days 18 hours has been quoted in various ways, at times even for the complete voyage. A careful calculation from her positions at noon on 7th and 8th February shows this to be her time from a point on the Newfoundland Grand Banks, at latitude 44°13'N, longitude 48°47'W, to Muckle Flugga, the island off the Shetland Islands with Britain's farthest north light. Only the clipper RED JACKET's 12-day crossing in January 1854 from Sandy Hook to Bell Buoy outside Liverpool was faster, and only two other large sailing ships have crossed from New York in less than 13 days. During one week of this crossing, LANCING logged 2,129 miles, at an average speed of nearly 13 knots: two records achieved by few other sailing ships. That this record was no fluke is borne out by Captain Olufsen's other wartime transatlantic crossings: 15 days between Halifax and Glasgow in 1916; 15 days between Quebec and Greenock in 1916; and in 1917 12 days between St Anne des Monts and Queenstown.

In 1918 Captain Olufsen was bound for Melbourne. After leaving Glasgow on 1st March he had to heave to in the Irish Sea, and when they were weighing anchor the carpenter, Carl Sommer, was lost overboard. From Belfast, Santos was reached in a rather slow 59 days, but from Santos to Melbourne LANCING took only 47.5 days. In Melbourne

Captain Olufsen became ill and was rushed to hospital, but recovered sufficiently to take her from Melbourne homeward bound on 29th August. However, during the morning of 16th September he complained of feeling ill again, and feared that 'he might die'. That evening tragedy struck: Captain Olufsen was lost overboard without anyone having seen how it occurred.

The mate, Mauritz Mathiassen, took over, and his times for the stages of the return voyage were: Melbourne to Barbados 69 days; New Orleans 16 days; and Queenstown 28 days. The final leg was completed in the worst weather that had up till then been recorded in the log-book. Whoever the skipper in charge after that, LANCING still produced some fine times. In 1919 Captain Peder Thv. Pedersen sailed from Cape Chat to Ardrossan in 16 days and from St Anne to Ardrossan in 15 days. In 1920 Captain Pedersen took her from Lamlash to Montevideo in 41 days, and in 1923 under Captain A. Larsen she could still cross the Atlantic in 15 days: what an achievement for a ship then 58 years old!

LANCING was reported overdue only twice in all her long life, but on both occasions she came in not many days after the report was issued. She maintained her first class rating unbroken from 1901. That she was still a sturdy ship was demonstrated in 1921 on her return voyage from Santos under Captain Pedersen when she survived first a grounding at Murray's Anchorage, Bermuda, and then, when fully loaded with Canadian timber, a collision with an ice-floe off the Newfoundland Banks.

LANCING believed to be at Melbourne. *[John Naylon collection]*.

LANCING's last voyages were spent bringing timber from Canada to Scotland, but between the end of 1922 and the beginning of 1924 there were occasions when freights were so poor that she was laid up in the Clyde. On 14th May 1924 she sailed again for Canada under her last captain, P. Hansen, who coaxed 58 miles from her in a watch and covered 283 miles in a day. On 4th August she sailed from Ardrossan to Canada for the last time. Her return crossing was as dramatic as any she had ever experienced, with hurricanes harrying her nearly all the way. It took her 34 days. At the end of 1924 she was sold to breakers in Genoa. She was towed to the Tuskar Light but sailed the rest of the way to Italy. Final proof of her quality was that even as scrap she fetched £6,250: only £50 below the price she had been bought for in 1901 - and this in the days before galloping inflation.

The great length of LANCING is particularly apparent when under bare poles. [Dr. Jurgen Meyer]

PUTTING THE RECORD STRAIGHT

Letters, additions, amendments and photographs relating to articles in any issues of *Record* are welcomed. Letters may be lightly edited.

The lively Arcs
I was interested in 'Milestones in Tramp Ship Development' by Alan McClelland in *Record 1* because in 1943 I was Chief Radio Officer of the LORD BYRON, formerly ARCGOW referred to in the article. The ARCTEES illustrated was similar but had a different deck arrangement and was slightly smaller. The identical sister ship was ARCWEAR, later LORD COCHRANE.

The article refers to these three ships proving 'extremely lively in adverse weather conditions'. I would say this was rather flattering. On one occasion in a beam sea, North Atlantic, wintertime, from the port side a wave cleared the funnel and took away the starboard lifeboat. Later we lost the main radio aerial trunk, swept away from the monkey island! F. SWIFT, Glyndeta, Bay View Road, East Looe, Cornwall PL13 1JW

The trials of LA PLAYA
I think that I can say with some certainty that the photograph of LA PLAYA on page 25 of *Record 5* was taken when the ship ran trials off Skelmorlie, in the Firth of Clyde. I have a copy of the same photo, taken, I believe, from the *Shipbuilding and Shipping Record* (1924). *The Motor Ship* (November 1923) and *The Shipbuilder* (January 1924) contain almost identical pictures, except that the ship is running in the opposite direction, against what looks like the same background. In all these photos of LA PLAYA the ship has the same trim and is flying identical flags from the mast-heads, bow and stern. *The Shipbuilder* reports that following trials off Skelmorlie, LA PLAYA made a five-day cruise round the coast of Ireland for those interested in the development of electric propulsion ships, so the photos could have been taken when on this cruise, but I am more inclined to think that they were the work of a professional photographer, commissioned to take trials photos.

Alan McClelland is fully justified in including LA PLAYA in his diesel-electric propulsion article because she was a pioneer in the application of such machinery to ships in which the auxiliary load forms a large proportion of the total electrical load. Today, similar conditions on board cruise ships, North Sea shuttle tankers, and icebreakers have led to the choice of diesel-electric machinery. Unfortunately, although LA PLAYA's electrical equipment was a success, the mechanical side was a disaster, and led to the ship not being a happy experience for the United Fruit Company.

The four original 4-cylinder Cammell Laird-Fullagar diesel generator engines suffered such frequent breakdowns that the owners opted to replace them in 1928 with four 4-cylinder Fiat engines, manufactured in Turin. But these engines were no more successful, and two years later they too were removed and LA PLAYA was laid up, engineless, at Mobile. There she remained for twelve years, until 1942. In that year her owners, who were probably desperate to replace war losses, decided to bring her back to life by fitting five 12-cylinder diesels to drive the electric generators. The new engines came from the General Electric Corporation in Cleveland, Ohio and were probably of a design developed for military purposes.

These new diesels apparently solved the problem because they were retained until the ship was broken up 26 years later. Although the very small space available for the diesel electric machinery must have severely limited the choice of replacement machinery; it must be rare for any ship to undergo three changes of engine type, and there cannot have been many ships which spent 12 years laid up with no means of propulsion.
JOHN B HILL, The Hollies, Wall, Hexham, Northumberland NE46 4EQ.

George Gardner, who has selected a number of photographs for Record *from the University of Glasgow archives, confirms that the picture of LA PLAYA was taken on the Skelmorlie measured mile on the Firth of Clyde. The misunderstanding arose from correspondence with another member of the University staff who was unaware of the Skelmorlie view and suggested one in another collection. Thanks also to Mike MacDonald for confirming the location.*

Pilot error
I note that in a recent *Record* the feature on diesel-electric propulsion has a photograph of the pilot cutter, EDMUND GARDNER. Whilst the technical description was fine, your comments were not strictly accurate. As I know you like your publication to be correct, it may be helpful if I put things in a truer perspective. I write as a retired Liverpool pilot with 38 years service, a member of the Committee of the Pilotage Authority of the Mersey Docks and Harbour Board (MDHB) and a one-time chairman of the Pilots' Association.

At the time of which you write, the pilots were self employed, sharing their pilotage earnings with their colleagues. Although they were not paid by the MDHB, the latter did own the cutters and a large percentage of the pilots' earnings were deducted to cover this and administration costs. Yes, time was often wasted waiting for ships at Lynas on Anglesey, but frequently we were waiting for ships whose owners or agents were well aware of their estimated time of arrival (ETA). However, because these owners/agents knew that, by law, pilots had to be available to offer a service in compulsory pilotage, they seldom thought it necessary to pass on ETA information - despite our pleas for them to do so. As pilots were fee-earners, wasted time meant wasted money. Our money. Added to this, bouncing around in bad weather for a couple of days was seldom as relaxing as you make it sound! The only rule-of-thumb we had for manning the pilot boat was the average number of men needed during each 24 hours. If more men were required later, individuals would be tacked on by train and taxi. The MDHB was well aware that over-manning was wasteful and that the answer was an enforceable ETA system. But they were also aware of the above-mentioned legal drawback. Eventually they bit the bullet and an ETA system was tried out. It became about 80% successful, and by dint of cajoling and threatening the owners and agents a proper system was established. Fortunately, the pilotage committee comprised shipowners and ships' agents as well as senior MDHB directors, and they helped to persuade the others. I can assure you that, although times were different from today, the MDHB committee members did not adopt the relaxed attitude which you implied.

The introduction of fast launches, first as tenders to the Bar Station boat and then as an experiment at Lynas, was certainly successful at Lynas. But to make Lynas into a shore station required the building of a jetty and accommodation: not cheap, but cheaper than a new cutter. In summary, your comments could have been presented more accurately. Your mention of 'well paid' was both questionable and unnecessary, doing justice neither to the pilots nor to the Mersey Docks and Harbour Board.
P.J.H. (JOHN) TEBAY, 13 Belmont Road, West Kirby, Wirral L48 5EY.

AMERICAN failure
Much as I am always delighted to find an unexpected tug, AMERICAN was not one! (*Record 4*, page 252)

In April 1860, on the back of poor service from the two existing companies, the Southampton, Isle of Wight & Portsmouth Improved Steam Boat Co. Ltd. was formed (and drove the other two to combine into what is now Red Funnel). They sought to bring two innovations to the Solent: firstly they had two paddlers built on the Thames with properly enclosed saloons 'designed to the American principle'. They also responded to customers' dissatisfaction with the use of towed barges for carriages and livestock by planning a new concept: a 'floating bridge' which used a larger, beamier vessel.

Consultant engineer to the new company was Charles Kernan of the Vulcan Iron Works at Millbrook, and it was from here that the appropriately-named AMERICAN was launched in October 1861. She was indeed very stubby, with dimensions of 130.3 x 25.6 x 8.3 feet (it took 70 years and the abandonment of paddles and steam for a Solent ferry to approach these proportions again - MEDINA of 1931). The central part of the deck was kept clear for carriages, horses, etc and there were slim saloons fore and aft of each paddle box; with bow and stern rudders she had been described as double-ended. Of her three registered owners (*Record 4*, page 252), Henry Pinnock was chairman of the Improved company and William Muntz was the principal shareholder and held a patent for the paddle wheel design used. It is difficult to imagine what she looked like from the available descriptions. The venture was a financial disaster - the heavy investment and fierce price war led to a joint service with the existing company by summer 1862 and bankruptcy a few months later. The passenger paddlers LORD OF THE ISLES and LADY OF THE LAKE were taken over by the opposition, but the AMERICAN (which may never have actually entered service) was left with the mortgagees James Mew & Robert Pinnock and presumably laid up. In 1868 they sold her to London merchant Bartholomew Hartley, who sold her on for conversion to a pontoon, but it looks as if her greater potential was realised and two years later she emerged from Edward Lindsay's Mushroom yard as ALLERWASH, with dimensions 131.0 x 25.3 x 11.6 feet.

I suppose that it is unlikely that any illustration of AMERICAN exists, unless perhaps Kernan or Muntz got something in one of the engineering journals.
DAVID ASPREY, 60 Barnstaple Road, Thorpe Bay, Southend-on-Sea, Essex SS1 3PA.

Every picture tells a different story
There were two steamships named MINISTER TAK VAN POORTVLIET. The photograph in *Record 5* (page 33) is of the first ship of this name built, with sister PROFESSOR BUYS, in 1891 by William Dobson and Co., Newcastle-upon-Tyne. In 1892 the two ships opened a freight service between Vlissingen and Hull for the Zeeuwsche Stoomvaart Maatschappij. The service and the two ships were taken over around two years later by Hollandsche Scheepvaart Maatschappij. Something serious happened to the first MINISTER TAK VAN POORTVLIET, for she disappears from *Lloyd's Register* about 1908: can the collision evident in your photograph have damaged her beyond economical repair?
JOHN BARTLETT, 6 Cottenham Park Road, London SW20 0RZ.

As penance for confusing these ships, the editor has gone back to Lloyd's Lists and their indexes, risking death-by-

microfilm in the process. The first MINISTER TAK VAN POORTVLIET certainly had some scrapes, and during December 1904 managed to come into contact with no less than three other ships on the foggy Humber. However, the damage seen in the photograph in Record 5 was undoubtedly due to a collision with the Bergen-registered steamer FALK (948/1904) near Sandhaile Buoy in the entrance to the Humber on 7th September 1905 whilst the Dutch ship was outward bound from Hull to Amsterdam. FALK docked at Grimsby with stem damage, but MINISTER TAK VAN POORTVLIET was much more seriously injured and had to be beached near the dock entrance at Grimsby with 'her starboard side smashed in aft of the engines.' After temporary repairs she docked at Hull on 11th September, and the photograph was almost certainly taken then before her damaged cargo was removed.

This accident did not end the career of MINISTER TAK VAN POORTVLIET (1), and she continued under the Dutch flag until 1909 when sold to James Halliday of Quebec who renamed her GENERAL WOLFE. She was less lucky in a subsequent collision. Whilst on a voyage from Seven Islands to Quebec with passengers and general cargo she sank on 28th June 1911 after hitting the ARANMORE (1,170/1890) off Murray Bay in the St. Lawrence. ARANMORE, an ex-Clyde Shipping steamer, was herself owned by James Halliday, which must have made for some interesting arguments.

Thanks also to Kevin O'Donoghue and Martin Lindenborn for pointing out that we had the wrong ship, and to George Robinson of Hull for taking the trouble to look in local papers for information on MINISTER TAK VAN POORTVLIET.

CHARLOIS at Coble Dene

In your excellent Record 5 I found on page 60 a mention of the tank steamer CHARLOIS. I thought you might be interested in the enclosed photograph of her copied from a lantern slide which turned up in a local antique dealers some years ago. I don't know when it was taken but the location was given as Coble Dene, which is on the north bank of the Tyne.

P.J. BARBER, South Tyneside College, St George's Avenue, South Shields, Tyne & Wear NE34 6ET.

Split opinions

Having perhaps, in a chance remark to the editors, initiated the comment in the caption to the KASSOS (Record 1) over the continuance of the split-superstructure configuration well into the motor ship era, I will pitch into the ongoing correspondence on this matter. The letter from Geoffrey Holmes in Record 5 suggests that this arrangement was beneficial to the trim of the vessel, which indeed endorses Alan McClelland's views in Record 2. There were, however, a number of vessels built to what is commonly referred to as the three-quarters aft arrangement, itself a means to that end, that still retained a split superstructure, and which would not support that theory. Ellerman's CITY OF MELBOURNE (later CITY OF CAPE TOWN) of 1957; the ARLINGTON COURT, built as late as 1962 and sold to Turnbull, Scott in 1964 when she became SOUTHGATE; and - most interestingly - the four M class cargo liners built for French Line in the late 1950s, are a few examples.

The disposition and configuration of the holds does not greatly differ between vessels having split or composite superstructure and the same principles of good cargo stowage, as outlined by Geoffrey Holmes, would appear to apply in both instances.

I tend to subscribe more to the reason put forward by Mr. Michael Matanos of the Kassos Steam Navigation Co. (Record 2) that the continuance of the split superstructure had, in fact, more to do with maintaining the segregation of the engineers from the deck officers (or vice versa, depending upon one's point of view). This was, perhaps, compounded by the blind adherance to old established

CHARLOIS lies in the Tyne off Coble Dene: a fascinating photograph showing an early tanker plus examples of a much earlier breed of fuel carrier, the East Coast collier brig. *P.J. Barber collection*

As mentioned in Paul Boot's letter, MICHIGAN (9,235/1959) (above) was one of four sisters built for Compagnie Générale Transatlantique with split superstructure placed in the three quarters aft position. Along with sisters MAGELLAN, MARYLAND, and MISSISSIPI she was given Doxford oil engines built under licence by her builders Ch. & At. De Provence at Port-de-Bouc near Marseilles. In 1976 MICHIGAN was sold to Singapore owners who renamed her BRANI ISLAND. She was broken up at Gadani Beach late in 1980.

ELDORITA enters Portreath *(left)*. [Ian Wilson collection]

design practices which bedevilled both shipbuilders and shipowners. The supposed benefits to navigation of having the bridge positioned further forward may well have helped to sustain this anachronism.

Whilst writing, could I also correct an error in Harry Hignett's letter in *Record 4*. It was Alexandra Towing's WALLASEY, not WILLOWGARTH, which - with a large tract of Liverpool Bay to drift in after she had been abandoned - managed to pass over the remains of PEGU and demolish the mast, causing a not inconsiderable amount of damage to herself in the process.
PAUL BOOT, 29 Meadowcroft, Barnston, Wirral, Merseyside L60 1UT

ELDORITA enters Portreath
I'm submitting the enclosed photograph of ELDORITA entering Portreath after reading about Captain Shaw's career *(Record 2)*. It was given to me by an ex-coasting skipper who was fascinated by Portreath and its tricky entrance.
IAN WILSON, 20 Windmill Road, Bangor BT20 5RA.

More weighty matters
Paul Boot's series on heavy lifts is most interesting and well presented, with superb photographs. As chief officer (the mate) of Blue Star Line's SOUTH AFRICA and AUSTRALIA STAR from 1962 to 1966, I had a personal interest in heavy lifters; so a few further observations may be acceptable.

Although Blue Star - along with Shaw Savill, Federal/New Zealand Shipping Company and Port Line - did indeed specialise in carrying refrigerated produce from Australia and New Zealand, the size and speed of their ships made them also ideal for carrying the vast amounts of general cargo from the UK and Europe on their outward voyages. By 1960 the export of locomotives and rolling stock had given way to the need for ships to be able carry large pieces of machinery in undivided loads, including boilers, stators for power stations, sugar mills, steel-making machinery, and even cement factories. As the weight of these items now surpassed the lifting capacities of the various floating and shoreside cranes at the ports visited, it was essential for the ships to load and unload with their own gear. As Paul Boot points out, the largest derricks fitted to the conference lines' vessels were in the 40-80 ton range, and to carry these lifts it became necessary to charter in ships from Clan Line, for example.

As the charter ship not only got the heavy lifts but all the other freight-earning items which went with the heavy lifts - right down to the nuts and bolts and fuse wire - Blue Star decided to have their own heavy lift ship. Because she happened to be in the right place at the right time, and had adequate stability, strength and electrical power, the steam turbine SOUTH AFRICA STAR was chosen and her new derrick, fitted by Howaldtswerke in Hamburg, came with what was at the time the largest unstayed mast afloat.

So profitable was she that a new, purpose-built heavy lifter, AUSTRALIA STAR, was ordered, with a derrick which for some time got us into the Guinness Book of Records as the world's largest, at 300 tons safe working load (SWL). The ship was built by Austin and Pickersgill at their Southwick Yard, Sunderland and during August 1965 she was towed over to Hamburg for installation of the derrick. I went over with her and stood by the installation at Stülcken's yard opposite St. Pauli.

One Sunday afternoon I was invited to attend the testing of a new derrick for one of the Hansa Line ships - a 120 ton derrick had been replaced with one of 140 ton SWL. The test was due to take place at 3.00 pm on a fine, almost calm afternoon. On climbing aboard I realised that they had not finished filling her water ballast tanks: their mate came to tell the captain that the double bottom tanks were still 'slack'. But it was 3.00 pm, time to test, and the mate went away, muttering. I was told that the vessel would list 13 degrees, and a large clinometer had been placed on the masthouse for all to see.

A water-filled barge weighing 154 tons (the required 10% overload) was moved alongside and the derrick's purchase hook attached. Lifting commenced. The ship heeled over more and more, until she was over the 13 degrees predicted, but the barge had still not lifted out of the water.

At 20 degrees the barge suddenly came clear, swinging the derrick hard over, collapsing it with a crash against the mast and denting itself in the process. Fortunately no one was hurt, but I realised that it was time for me to leave, as 'Donners und Blitzens' were flying like shrapnel. Next day the shipyard manager said, with a wry grin, 'Now, Herr Kinghorn, you know what not to do!' It had been a marvellous lesson in the absolute necessity of having all your tanks 'pressed up' (completely full) and how, with a Stülcken derrick, you must never allow even one of your twin topping lifts to slack, because this will cause the derrick to collapse. With no guys to hold the hook, the swivels to which the topping lifts are attached atop the masts will swivel uncontrollably, with what could be disastrous results!

Incidentally, a Stülcken derrick has four, not two, controlling winches, because each topping lift and both ends of the fall purchase need a winch. The four winches of the AUSTRALIA STAR were mounted one over the other, two each inside her massive Stülcken masts which were 12 feet in diameter at the base. Cabs near the top of each 70-foot high mast both had two winch controls, and the winch drives, one in each cab, were directed by the mate in charge, on deck with a microphone. A typical order would be 'starboard topping lift up on four, port topping lift up on three, both purchases up on two'. Exacting! Dockers, even Australian wharfies, were quite happy to let the ship's people work the derrick - after we had made the first lift look particularly difficult.

By the way, the SOUTH AFRICA STAR was not scrapped in 1967, although she was taken to Japan with that intention. Although, as part of the scrapping order, the 180 ton derrick was dropped by the mate (not me, by then) to render it unfit for further use, the ship was fitted with a standard mast and run by C.Y. Tung's Orient Overseas Line, with her sister ship RHODESIA STAR. Both were finally scrapped at Taiwan in 1972, at almost 30 years old. Not bad for Woolworths carriers.

CAPTAIN A.W. KINGHORN, 15 Kendal Avenue, Cullercoats, North Shields, Tyne & Wear NE30 3AQ.

Testing the AUSTRALIA STAR's derrick to 300 tons at Hamburg during October 1965. [Captain AW Kinghorn]

SOUTH AFRICA STAR unloading part of a steel-making plant from Middlesbrough at Whyalla. *[Captain AW Kinghorn]*

SOURCES AND ACKNOWLEDGEMENTS

Photographs are from the collection of John Clarkson unless otherwise credited. We thank all who gave permission for their photographs to be used, and are particularly grateful to George Scott, to David Whiteside and Tony Smith of the World Ship Photo Library; and to the museums and institutions listed for help in finding photographs.

In researching captions, sources have included the *Registers* of William Schell and Tony Starke, *Lloyd's Register, Lloyd's Confidential Index, Lloyd's War Losses, Mercantile Navy Lists,* and *Marine News.* Use of the facilities of the World Ship Society's Central Record, the Guildhall Library and Lloyd's Register of Shipping are gratefully acknowledged. Particular thanks also to William Schell, Louis Loughran and John Bartlett for information and to Heather Fenton for editorial services.

Guinness
Terry O'Conallain kindly read the first draft and added much useful information. A brief account of the company's shipowning appeared in the December 1960 edition of Sea Breezes. Also consulted were the *Journal of the Brewery History Society* No. 39 (March 1984) and No. 72 (June 1993), kindly suplied by Keith Duke, *Shipbuilding & Shipping Record, 15th March 1974* and *Modern Ships* by R Carpenter (MAP Ltd., Hemel Hempstead, 1970).

Palmers
Thanks for valuable assistance to Dr. Richard F. Palmer, Peter Thomas, Roy Fenton, Cork Harbourmaster Captain P. Farnan, and Sean O'Mahony.

Whaler conversions
Among the many sources used, the ones most pertinent to whaling are: *Men & Whales* by Richard Ellis (Robert Hale 1992, London), *The History of Modern Whaling* by JN Tønnessen & AO Johnsen (C.Hurst & Co. 1982, London), *Hvalfangsten* by Dag Bakka Jr (Krohn Johansen Forlag 1992, Larvik), *From 70*

North to 70 South by Graeme Somner (Christian Salvesen 1984, Edinburgh), *Salvesen of Leith* by Wray Vamplew (Scottish Academic Press 1975, Edinburgh), *Whale Factory Ships* by John G Callis (*Ships Illustrated* July and August 1967), *The World's Tankers* by Laurence Dunn (Adlard Coles 1956), *Ships at Grytviken* by Nigel Bonner (South Georgia Whaling Museum 1993), *Stewart Island's Kaipipi Shipyard and the Ross Sea Whalers* by JPC Watt, *Catchers & Corvettes* by John H Harland (Jean Boudriot Publication 1992) and *The World's Fishing Fleets* by Edward Paget-Tomlinson (in *The Golden Age of Shipping*, Conway Maritime Press 1994, London).

Many thanks for help with photographs and information from: Laurence Dunn, Roy Fenton, Ambrose Greenway, Peter Jeftha, Paul Louden-Brown, George Mortimore, John Naylon, Kevin O' Donoghue, William Schell, Jimmy Smith and Graeme Somner.

Connell Brothers Ltd.
Imperial War Museum; Scottish Record Office (file BT2/4661). Mr C.R. Connell has been most helpful.

Wanstead to Woodford
Contemporary journals contained much on these ships, see for instance *Marine News*, 1949, page 143. Watts Watts Line's splendid book on the three ships was very kindly loaned by Ian Wells. Thanks also to Tony Blackler and Ken Bottoms, who have researched the company, and to Warwick Foote for pointing out how interesting these ships were. The later careers of the ships are dealt with in the excellent *Beancaker to Boxboat* by HW Dick & SA Kentwell (Nautical Association of Australia Inc, Canberra, 1988).

Under two flags
Thanks to Richard Cornish for pointing out the two flags in this photograph. Details of the BEGONIA's career are from *The Gorthon Shipping Companies* 1915-1985 by KA Axelson & T Johannesson (World Ship Society, Kendal, 1985), *The Dannebrog Fleet* 1883-1993 by Søren Thorsøe et al (Dannebrog Rederi, Rungsted, 1993) and *Lloyd's Register*.

WANSTEAD TO WOODFORD
Roy Fenton

The post-war years of British shipping are littered with ships heralded as innovative and trend-setting, but which were sold after a relatively short service due to unforeseen changes in trade. It is refreshing, however, to be able to chronicle one small group that was both innovative and did fulfil their promise, and which spent two decades earning money for their original owners. These were the Watts, Watts motorships WANSTEAD, WENDOVER and WOODFORD, delivered from the Caledon yard in Dundee during 1949 and 1950.

The ships were built for the Watts, Watt's service from Montreal and other Canadian ports to Antwerp, Rotterdam and Hamburg, a service had been begun in 1946 under the name Watts Watts Line, and for whom Cunard acted as Canadian agents. However, the ships were to spend much of their later careers on charter to or owned by other companies in the cargo liner trade. Ironically, these services had little requirement for the special features with which the ships were designed to meet the rigours of the North Atlantic winter, including ice-strengthening and a stability which took into account the weight of ice which was likely to form on decks and superstructure.

W for well-appointed

The feature of WANSTEAD and her sisters which excited most attention in the technical press was the standard of crew accommodation. British ships in general, and especially those of so-called 'tramp' operators, had a dismal record in terms of catering for the comfort of their crews. Indeed, British crews allocated to US-built standard ships during the Second World War were often impressed by the standard of accommodation fitted, which is all the more surprising as the Liberties were built to an essentially British design.

Watts, Watts were, in later years at least, an exception amongst shipowners in caring about the lot of their seafarers. Edmund Watts read a paper on the subject of crew accommodation in tramp ships to the Institution of Naval Architects in April 1949. He began by painting a picture of conditions in the 1920s. The ratings lived in the forecastle, sleeping in double-tiered bunks, and eating where they slept. Whereas it was not far to carry the captain's and navigating officers' food from galley to saloon, to get it to the engineer's mess a 30 foot walk was usually needed, mostly in the open. And the walk from galley to forecastle was, he maintained, long enough to ruin any food. He was not impressed with the usual positioning of the galley at the fore end of the engineroom casing where the ship took most water. Watts then contrasted conditions in his own company's recent ships, beginning with the

BLACKHEATH of 1936. In this ship the seamen and firemen's accommodation had been placed in the poop rather than in the forecastle. In the later ships of the TOTTENHAM class, accommodation had been moved amidships. This gave the crew better air and light, and placed them nearer to the galley and to their work. However, Watts admitted that the crew did not always like this, and preferred to be in the poop by themselves, and not close to the officers!

In Watt's new ship WANSTEAD, all accommodation was amidships, the majority being in the 'tween decks and trunked around numbers 3 and 4 hatches. A single cabin was provided for most members of the crew, the exceptions being the ordinary seamen and boys. There were no outside cabins, the accommodation in the 'tween decks being so arranged that recreational galleries occupied both port and starboard sides, with cabins opening inboard from these. The oblong windows in the hull sides of the ships show just how far these extended. Perhaps in deference to the crew's sensitivities about being too close to the officers, their cabins were grouped to starboard with the deck and engineering officers' cabins to port. The crew had a cafeteria (one of the first in a British ship) in the 'tween decks, whilst the officers had their dining room a deck higher: separate provisions which now seem wasteful but which were considered essential in the late 1940s. It was claimed that WANSTEAD was the first ship in which the deck and engineering officers and the crew had been placed together in one structure and on one deck. Edmund Watts was evidently very proud of the design, to the extent that the exploded view reproduced here was commissioned and printed, and a 40-page booklet was published by Watts, Watts themselves.

Cold comfort

The cold climate in which the ships were intended to trade is reflected in the hull's ice-strengthening and other details of their design. The prominent knuckle in the hull at bow and stern was said to improve heavy weather behaviour by increasing buoyancy, and is also credited to Edmund Watts: it was subsequently referred to as the 'Watts knuckle'. Parts of the accommodation which needed water - the galley, laundry, wash places and toilets - were grouped around the engineroom casing whose heat helped prevent the plumbing from freezing. The ventilation system was inspired by Edmund Watt's experience of coal mines, the air being exhausted by four discharge fans which fulfilled the same function as an upcast shaft in a mine. The idea was to eliminate the sweating along the ship's side due to the coolness of the outside air. Even more considerate was a superstructure design which made it unnecessary for the crew to go on deck during the

The layout of the accommodation in WANSTEAD-class ships

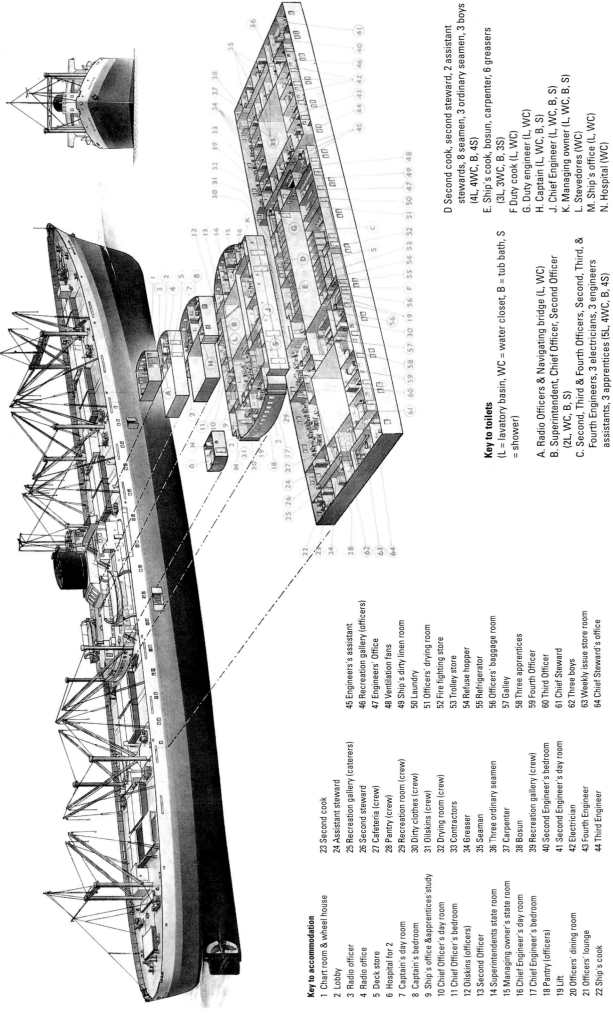

Key to accommodation

1 Chart room & wheel house
2 Lobby
3 Radio officer
4 Radio office
5 Deck store
6 Hospital for 2
7 Captain's day room
8 Captain's bedroom
9 Ship's office &apprentices' study
10 Chief Officer's day room
11 Chief Officer's bedroom
12 Oilskins (officers)
13 Second Officer
14 Superintendents state room
15 Managing owner's state room
16 Chief Engineer's day room
17 Chief Engineer's bedroom
18 Pantry (officers)
19 Lift
20 Officers' dining room
21 Officers' lounge
22 Ship's cook

23 Second cook
24 Assistant steward
25 Recreation gallery (caterers)
26 Second steward
27 Cafeteria (crew)
28 Pantry (crew)
29 Recreation room (crew)
30 Dirty clothes (crew)
31 Oilskins (crew)
32 Drying room (crew)
33 Contractors
34 Greaser
35 Seaman
36 Three ordinary seamen
37 Carpenter
38 Bosun
39 Recreation gallery (crew)
40 Second Engineer's bedroom
41 Second Engineer's day room
42 Electrician
43 Fourth Engineer
44 Third Engineer

45 Engineers's assistant
46 Recreation gallery (officers)
47 Engineers' Office
48 Ventilation fans
49 Ship's dirty linen room
50 Laundry
51 Officers' drying room
52 Fire fighting store
53 Trolley store
54 Refuse hopper
55 Refrigerator
56 Officers' baggage room
57 Galley
58 Three apprentices
59 Fourth Officer
60 Third Officer
61 Chief Steward
62 Three boys
63 Weekly issue store room
64 Chief Steward's office

D Second cook, second steward, 2 assistant stewards, 8 seamen, 3 ordinary seamen, 3 boys (4L, 4WC, B, 4S)
E Ship's cook, bosun, carpenter, 6 greasers (3L, 3WC, B, 3S)
F Duty cook (L, WC)
G Duty engineer (L, WC)
H Captain (L, WC, B, S)
J Chief Engineer (L, WC, B, S)
K Managing owner (L, WC, B, S)
L Stevedores (WC)
M Ship's office (L, WC)
N Hospital (WC)

Key to toilets

(L = lavatory basin, WC = water closet, B = tub bath, S = shower)

A. Radio Officers & Navigating bridge (L, WC)
B. Superintendent, Chief Officer, Second Officer (2L, WC, B, S)
C. Second, Third & Fourth Officers, Second, Third, & Fourth Engineers, 3 electricians, 3 engineers assistants, 3 apprentices (5L, 4WC, B, 4S)

normal course of a voyage. Those handling mooring ropes and driving the winches in port also received some protection from covered structures. Control gear for the winches was so arranged that the operators had a full view of the hatch and the load, another unusual feature at the time. Steel hatchcovers were fitted, and to maximise speed of operation all but one of these were split in two and slid athwartship to open. An interesting feature was two sets of shell doors fitted on each side of the hull to facilitate loading cars and packaged cargo in the lower 'tween decks. The uppermost deck - the shelter deck - was the main strength deck and was suitable for carrying deck cargoes such as logs.

The ships were built to operate at about 15 knots, being driven by 5-cylinder Doxford two-stroke oil engines of 6,250 indicated horse power. These were built by Scott's Shipbuilding and Engineering Co. Ltd. of Greenock.

Charter and sale

The Watts Watts Line did not prosper greatly, but the company found it possible to charter their ships to liner companies, and the fleet list entries below catalogue the sisters' major stints on charter to Port Line and Lamport and Holt.

In the 1960s the China Navigation Co. Ltd. was recovering from the loss of its traditional China coasting business, and was profiting from the growing trade between Australia and South East Asia. In 1964 they demise chartered and renamed the three Watts, Watts sisters. WANLIU and WENCHOW replaced China Navigation ships on the indirect

service from Australia to Japan via Manila, Hong Kong, Taiwan and Okinawa, whilst WOOSUNG operated a direct service alongside China Navigation's TSIENTSIN and TSINGTAO. They were successful enough for the Hong Kong company to exercise an option to purchase them in 1969. The ships were noted for their excellent bale capacity when carrying the Australian wool clip: presumably this resulted from their design for the Canadian trade which ensured they were suitable for forest products which occupied a relatively large volume for their weight.

In the mid-1970s China Navigation containerised much of its Australia-Japan trade, and the three Ws were sold. Each found a different Asian buyer who squeezed a couple more years of service from the ships, all of which were broken up during 1978. Judged by their longevity they had been a very successful design, serving their original owners for almost twenty years, and trading for almost three decades in total. Reports suggest that they were also appreciated by their crews.

Beginning with WINDSOR of 1952, Watts, Watts built three tramps with similar hull forms, but with the accommodation in the superstructure. Then came another striking and innovative design, the remarkable WEYBRIDGE class of 1958, which repeated the accommodation arrangement of WANSTEAD although with a very different layout. However, the relatively early sales of the WEYBRIDGE class suggest they were by no means as successful as the WANSTEADs, which represent a major landmark in the development of cargo ship design.

Class list

1. WANSTEAD 1949-1969
O.N.183130 5,664g 2,746n 475.8 x 64.3 x 22.2 feet
Doxford-type oil engines 5-cyl. 2SCSA by Scott's Shipbuilding and Engineering Co. Ltd., Greenock; 6,250 IHP, 15 knots.
10.5.1949: Launched by the Caledon Shipbuilding and Engineering Co. Ltd., Dundee (Yard No. 469).
10.1949: Completed for the Britain Steamship Co. Ltd. (Watts, Watts and Co. Ltd., managers), London as WANSTEAD.
1957: Renamed PORT WANSTEAD whilst on charter to Port Line Ltd., London.
1960: Renamed WANSTEAD.
1963: Renamed RAEBURN whilst on charter to Lamport & Holt Line Ltd.,
4.1964: Renamed WANSTEAD.
1964: Renamed WANLIU whilst on demise charter to the China Navigation Co. Ltd., Hong Kong.
1969: Sold to the China Navigation Co. Ltd., Hong Kong.
1.1975: sold to the Maldives Shipping Ltd., Male, Maldive Islands and renamed MALDIVE EXPLORER.
11.6.1978: Arrived at Gadani Beach to be broken up.

2. WENDOVER 1950-1969
O.N.183183 5,664g 2,746n 475.8 x 64.3 x 22.2 feet
Doxford-type oil engines 5-cyl. 2SCSA by Scott's Shipbuilding and Engineering Co. Ltd., Greenock; 6,250 IHP, 15 knots.
23.8.1949: Launched by the Caledon Shipbuilding and Engineering Co. Ltd., Dundee (Yard No. 470).

2.1950: Completed for the Britain Steamship Co. Ltd. (Watts, Watts and Co. Ltd., managers), London as WENDOVER.
4.1964: Renamed WENCHOW whilst on demise charter to the China Navigation Co. Ltd., Hong Kong.
1969: Sold to the China Navigation Co. Ltd., Hong Kong.
7.1975: Sold to Pacific International Lines (Pte.) Ltd., Singapore and renamed KOTA SUBUR.
30.10.1978: Arrived up at Gadani Beach to be broken up by S.Z. Enterprise Ltd.

3. WOODFORD 1950-1969
O.N.183281 5,664g 2,746n 475.8 x 64.3 x 22.2 feet
Doxford-type oil engines 5-cyl. 2SCSA by Scott's Shipbuilding and Engineering Co. Ltd., Greenock; 6,250 IHP, 15 knots.
21.11.1949: Launched by the Caledon Shipbuilding and Engineering Co. Ltd., Dundee (Yard No. 471).
7.1950: Completed for the Britain Steamship Co. Ltd. (Watts, Watts and Co. Ltd., managers), London as WOODFORD.
1963: Renamed ROSETTI whilst on charter to Lamport & Holt Ltd.,
1964: Renamed WOODFORD.
4.1964: Renamed WOOSUNG whilst on demise charter to the China Navigation Co. Ltd., Hong Kong.
1969: Sold to the China Navigation Co. Ltd., Hong Kong.
4.1976: Sold to Guan Guan Enterprising (Hong Kong) Ltd., Singapore and renamed NEW DRAGON.
30.5.1978: Left Karachi for Shanghai to be broken up.

WANSTEAD and her sisters were hardly beauties. A squat superstructure (belying the extent of accommodation in the 'tween decks), topped by a large funnel, together with goalposts and kingposts rather than real masts robbed them of much grace. However, with the forecastle eliminated she had a flush-decked hull reminiscent of the Liberties and which was not unattractive, with the shelter deck (but not the main deck) having a good degree of sheer.
For a charter to Port Line, WANSTEAD took the slightly risible name PORT WANSTEAD; the north east London district after which she was named having no pretensions whatsoever to being a port. PORT WANSTEAD is seen here at Brisbane (opposite page, top left). In 1963 she carried the name RAEBURN for a Lamport & Holt charter (opposite page, top right).

On charter to, and later owned by, China Navigation Co. Ltd. WANSTEAD became WANLIU. The photograph bottom left opposite shows several interesting features, including two apparently canvas-covered boxes, one abaft the funnel and one right astern. Could they have been for conveying animals, possibly racehorses to and from Hong Kong? WANLIU's funnel colours are believed to be those of Asia Australia Express Ltd., a company formed in 1973 by Royal Interocean Lines and China Navigation Co. Ltd., both of whose houseflags are flying in this New Zealand view. Under her final name MALDIVE EXPLORER funnel colours became simply black (bottom right). *[This page: Fotoflite incorporating Skyfotos; opposite page top left: V.H. Young & L.A. Sawyer]*

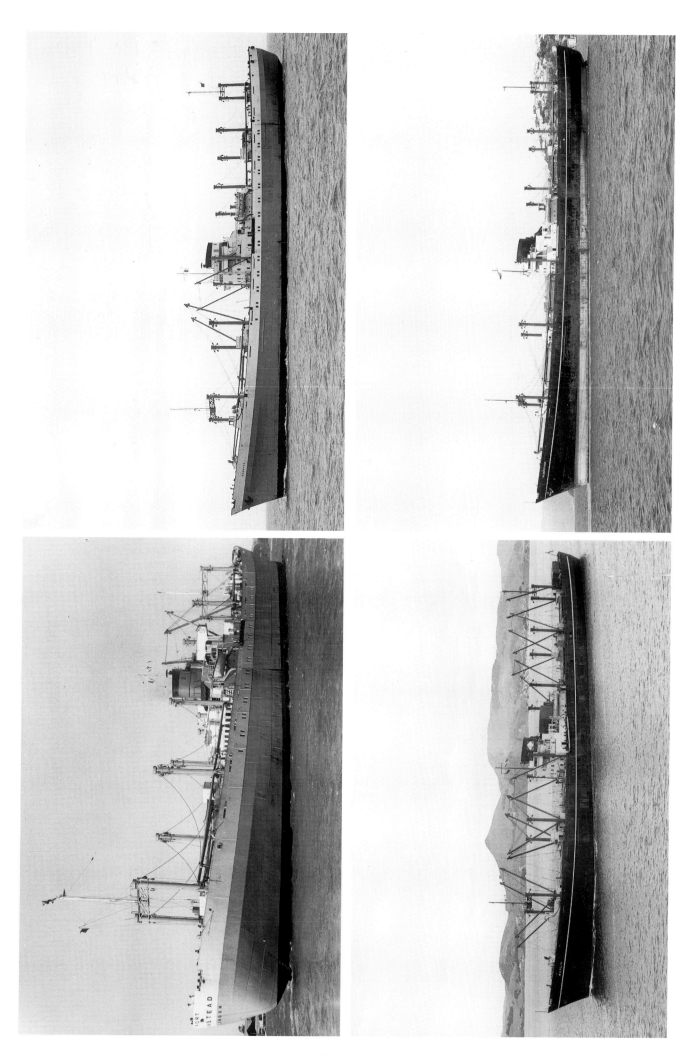

Watts, Watts' ships are often described as being named after suburbs or districts of London, but after the company decided that only names beginning with the letter W were to be allowed, this definition was widened. WENDOVER, for instance, took her name from a delightful small town on the scarp slope of the Chilterns, well out of London.

A change from the black funnel (opposite page) to red with black rings and top (this page top) indicates that WENDOVER was on charter to Port Line in this dramatically-lit shot.

The centre view of WENDOVER as WENCHOW on 5th January 1974 shows that at some time in her career she had received a massive addition to her foremast. Can any reader explain this, which seems not to have any connection with the derricks? Another detail change is the addition of light lattice masts on the bridge wings.

Final owners of the ship were Pacific International Lines, who renamed her KOTA SUBUR as seen in the bottom photograph taken when she was anchored off her home port of Singapore in April 1976. [Opposite: Fotoflite incorporating Skyfotos; this page top: A. Duncan; bottom: V.H. Young & L.A. Sawyer]

The photograph of WOODFORD at a North American port in 1957 emphasises the fine sheer of her hull (opposite page top).

For charter to Lamport & Holt in 1963, WOODFORD became ROSETTI (opposite middle).

The class looked very well in the restrained colours of China Navigation Co. Ltd. In an Australian port in 16th January 1965, WOOSUNG ex WOODFORD was still on charter to the Hong Kong company and still had a plain black funnel (opposite bottom). All three of the WANSTEAD class were broken up within a few months of each other during the latter part of 1978. On this page NEW DRAGON, as WOODFORD had become, rides at anchor in Singapore Roads on 10th June 1978 during her final voyage from Karachi to Shanghai shipbreakers. The stem damage evident here may have hastened her end. *[Opposite middle: A. Duncan; this page: Table Bay Underway Shipping]*

UNDER TWO FLAGS – AT ONCE?

Observers of contemporary shipping are not surprised when a ship, and particularly a German one, flies the flag of one country whilst being registered at a port in an entirely different country. However, what are we to make of a ship flying two national ensigns at once?

The vessel in question is the BEGONIA (1,806/1890), photographed by Basil Feilden in the Mersey, and at her stern fly two flags, one above the other (inset). The upper one appears to be Finnish - a dark cross on a pale ground, but the way contemporary photographic emulsion 'reads' colour could conceivably make it a Swedish flag, with a yellow cross on blue. Below this flutters a tricolour, vertically divided. Ownership of BEGONIA gives few clues as to the meaning of this. She took the name in 1923 when sold by one Swedish owner to another. New owner was Rederi A/B Aurora, one of several companies managed by the Gorthon/Börjesson family, and in the photograph she carries their funnel colours. In 1934 she was sold to Alfred

Kalm of Tallinn without change of name. BEGONIA remained under the Estonian flag until she became embroiled in the invasion of Norway in April 1940 and was scuttled after being damaged in the Sognefjord. The photograph is, unfortunately, undated, but the Gorthon funnel points to it being taken between 1923 and 1934, during which time she was resolutely Swedish. Can any reader offer an explanation of the two flags?

BEGONIA began life during 1890 at Laing's yard in Sunderland, where she was built as AROS for London owners, Newman and Dale. In 1900 she was sold to Denmark as SILKEBORG, becoming an A.P. Möller ship when renamed ELISABETH MAERSK in 1914. After a few months as the Danish GULBORGSUND she was sold to Sweden in 1920 and became ANNA. A further interesting feature apparent in the photograph is the lack of any substantial structure amidships around the funnel: daylight is visible beneath the boat deck.

BOWATERS FOLLOW UP

The article on Bowaters in *Record 5* has caused considerable interest, and we are pleased to follow it up with some further photographs kindly supplied by Bill Schell.

LIVERPOOL LOYALIST *(top)*
Swan, Hunter and Wigham Richardson Ltd., Newcastle-upon-Tyne; 1932, 1,416g, 248 feet
United States Coastguard photographs provide an invaluable record of ships in wartime, this shot of LIVERPOOL LOYALIST being dated 16th February 1942. She was one of a number of ships built by Swans for Canada, a subject we intend to return to in a future *Record*. Her original manager was Frank K. Warren of Halifax, Nova Scotia for whom she ran as ZENDA on a service from New Brunswick and Nova Scotia ports up the St. Lawrence to Montreal and Toronto. In 1941 she was bought by the Mersey Paper Co. Ltd., a company who owes its place in this story to their acquisition by Bowaters in 1956. ZENDA was placed under the ownership of the Liverpool Loyalist Shipping Co. Ltd. and the management of Markland Shipping Co. Ltd. Renaming as LIVERPOOL LOYALIST followed in 1942, the Canadian Government evidently being more liberal about wartime renamings than the British authorities. The paper company soon sold her once hostilities had finished and in 1946 she became the Norwegian ALA. In 1951 the steamer was sold to the Merchant Steam Navigation Co. Ltd., Bombay and renamed SAGAR PRABHA. They retained her until she was broken up in Bombay in November 1960. *[Eric Johnson/Wm. Schell]*

NORTH BROOK *(centre)*
McDougall-Duluth Co., Duluth, Minnesota; 1919, 2,373gt, 251 feet
The story of NORTH BROOK, something of a distress purchase in 1940, was told in

Record 5, but this photograph is the best that has yet turned up. A further United States Coastguard photograph, it was taken on 12th July 1942. NORTH BROOK was sold by Bowater's Newfoundland Pulp and Paper Mills Ltd. very soon after the war, so she probably ran as NORTH BROOK only in grey paint. *[Eric Johnson/Wm. Schell]*

MARKLAND (1) *(bottom)*
Earle's Shipbuilding and Engineering Co. Ltd., Hull; 1929, 4,454gt, 327 feet
This photograph completes the story of MARKLAND, delivered to the Mersey Shipping Co. Ltd. to coincide with the opening of the mill owned by the Mersey Paper Co. Ltd. As LIVERPOOL ROVER she survived long enough to carry Bowaters colours. *[R. Scozza/Wm. Schell]*

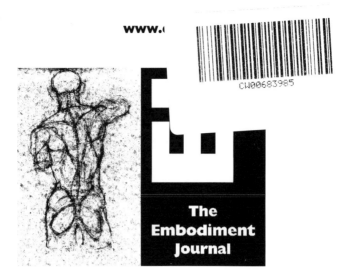

www.(

The
Embodiment
Journal

ISBN: 978-0-9567799-4-6

A copy of this book has been deposited with the British Library.

Published by Warriors of Love (WOL) Publishing

The Embodiment Journal

Volume One

Winter-Spring 2015

Contributors:

Francis Briers is the founder and editor of The Embodiment Journal. He is a Senior Consultant with a boutique leadership consultancy and one of the lead trainers on the Embodied Facilitator Course which is the first European home-grown training for business trainers and coaches to learn to work with the body and for 'body people' to learn how to work in business. Francis has been exploring the mind-body connection for 20 years and his studies include a 3rd Dan black belt in Kodo Ryu Karate, being a certified Uzazu embodiment coach, and a degree from one of the UK's top drama schools. He has developed his own approach to embodiment working in detail with posture called 'Somatic Presence.'

Find out more about the Embodied Facilitator Course at: www.embodiedfacilitator.com

John Tuite taught in challenging London schools for 18 years, serving on leadership teams in four of them. He was also an Advanced Skills Teacher. John is now a founder of the Centre for Embodied Wisdom, a qualified teacher of Leadership Embodiment, and a student of Wendy Palmer. Prior to this he worked as a builder, an arborist and a councilor. He is also the Senior Instructor of Grandmaster Han Kim Sen of Southern Shaolin Five Ancestor and Wuji. He has practiced within this tradition since 1974.

www.centreforembodiedwisdom.com

Nancy Shanteau spends her time in Nevada County, CA offering Skills for Change coaching to individuals, couples, families and groups. She recently co-authored "Access to Power: a Radical Approach for Changing Your Life" and she leads trainings in Skills for Change for individuals seeking radical life transformation and a certification program for coaches, therapists, and other practitioners. Through analysis of power, embodied practices, and freedom from internalized oppression, she helps people change their lives and achieve their dreams.

More information can be found at www.nancyshanteau.com

Beka Card is teacher of Embodied Awareness including Yoga & Somatics, Meditation, Earth & Nature Connection, Spirit-based practices, Soul~Crafting, Poetry, and Ceremony. She runs retreats, workshops, and offers one-to-one work. You can find more of her poetry at: http://wildcardme.tumblr.com/

Clare Myatt, LL.B., M.A. specialises in treating trauma and addiction. Initially licensed in California as a Marriage and Family Therapist in 1998 and subsequently certified by Strozzi Institute as a Master Somatic Coach, the first in the UK, Clare is a therapeutic-coach working somatically. She sees clients in London and Birmingham, and internationally using the web.

www.claremyatt.co.uk

Tess Howell is an artist, art therapist, dance producer, dancer, costumier, and ceremonialist. She is passionate about creativity for transformation and inspiration and as a way to connect with self and source. She is a 5 Rhythms teacher and instigator of the Wild Grace project, taking movement and dance out into nature, and the Rites of Passage women's leadership program in Brighton, UK.

www.creative-journey.com/#/the-team/4586411165

Charlie Birch is the CEO and Founder of Being Human Ally Inc., a business consulting service that specializes in burnout recovery and prevention. She is also Vice President of Climate & Culture Connection, a consulting firm that provides positive self leadership in the school system. Lastly, she is the creator of the Super Charge Your

Life Blog, an experiential practice based blog that promotes integrated positive psychology. As a chronic pain survivor and a recovering workaholic, Charlie's mission is to empower all humans to become their own greatest healer, resource, and ally. Charlie lives her life in conscious rebellion to the norm. She dose not believe life has to be a struggle. Rather she believes that struggle is a gift to fuel growth and transformation; that humans must welcome struggle but not accept it as a way of life. Charlie aspires to live in a world full of joy, play, love, and community. Previously, Charlie has worked as a dance teacher, choreographer, behavioral modification specialist, youth mentor, psychiatric crisis responder, and life coach. In her down time, Charlie enjoys being with nature, road trips, international adventures, deep conversations, live music, dancing, meditation, snowboarding, and beach bum days.

For more information about Charlie visit www.CharlieBirchProjects.com

Anouk Brack, MSc in biology is an expert in embodying integral leadership for sustainability. She founded the Experience Integral Foundation, is executive coach and Leadership Embodiment trainer.

She welcomes connection at www.linkedin.com/in/anoukbrack

Introduction - Francis Briers

It is a great joy to be writing this introductory editorial for of the embodiment journal. In so many ways it feels like this has been a long time coming, both for me personally and in some ways for the field of embodiment. I wanted to create a place where the leading thinking on embodiment could be shared openly both between practitioners and as an introduction for those newly interested in the field. Like so many things the field of embodiment has the potential to become a divided community separated by areas of interest, traditions, teachers, and theories of best practice. While I would hope for there to be some common areas, especially in terms of best practice, my intention in founding this journal is to create a "nondenominational" space to share our thinking and collectively evolve the field both in terms of how we do what we do and how widely the gifts of embodiment can be shared for the good of individuals, society, humankind, and indeed the Planet.

If you are new to embodiment, reading this hoping for an Introduction, what I also wanted to offer was an answer to the often asked question: "What is embodiment?" In some ways that's an easy thing to answer, as my friend and colleague Mark Walsh says "it's how you are!" We are beings living in bodies and regardless of your degree of cerebral focus or spiritual beliefs, everything we experience, we experience through our bodies. However, this answer may not be the most helpful in understanding what the primary concerns are in the field of embodiment. A definition which I enjoy and have been finding is a good 'way in' for people draws on two ancient Greek words. The first is 'Sarx.' This is the Greek word for the body referring to it as a piece of meat. I would suggest that this is the socially normal way of relating to our bodies and even people who "take care of their bodies" tend to treat it as a thing to be beautified, or a vehicle to be made more efficient. For many of us our bodies become little more than taxi's to take our brains to meetings. I hear many people express concern about the way advertising often objectifies our bodies, especially the way it objectifies women. I think that this is part of how our mechanical relationship with our bodies is culturally sustained but in another way whatever story the media might tell, we are so busy objectifying our own bodies I wonder how much difference it makes. The ancient Greek word 'Soma' which is the origin of the word Somatics - another word for embodiment used by practitioners - refers to experiencing the body as a lived experience. It is subjective not objective and encompasses the fact that how we inhabit our bodies shapes the way we see the world, the way we think, the way we feel, and the way we relate to each other. In a way that brings us full circle back to Mark's definition: "embodiment is how you are" so... If you want to relate to your body as more than a brain taxi, more than a machine to be made efficient, more than an accessory to be beautified, then you are in the right place. Dive in and enjoy!

This first volume has been blessed with an abundance of brilliant thinking and deep experience in cultivating somatic awareness and embodied wisdom. I want to take a moment to express my immense gratitude to all those who have helped to bring this journal into being. You'll see different perspectives and ways of working expressed and described - that is deliberate. There is no single 'right' way of working with the body or practicing embodiment. There are some principles of rigorous and ethical practice but many methods and philosophies. I think that is healthy and seek here to support the diversity not contain or edit it away. I invite you to explore widely and deeply here and elsewhere and shape your own opinions - inspired perhaps by the rich wisdom of others.

I hope you enjoy reading these articles as much as I have.

An Editor's note: In several of the following articles an embodiment practice 'Centring' (or 'Centering' in the American spelling) is mentioned. There is some description of this which will hopefully describe it in a useful enough manner if you are not already familiar with some kind of centring practice. There are many ways to 'centre' but if you want to know more then experiencing it may be most useful. You can find some audio recordings to talk you through two centring methods at:

http://www.fudoshin.org.uk/free-resources/exercises/grounding-and-centring/

Strength and Aliveness in Teaching - John Tuite

It is easier to say "You've got to be tough" than to say "You've got to be sensitive" in many school staffrooms.

This is understandable.

We need strength to be a teacher. Facing a challenging class requires a fundamental courage and resolution. Each day, each hour, we point our determination at whatever stands in our way. We rally our mind, re-set the tone of our limbs, the shape of our face, the width of our throat, to match the pressure we face. It's part of the nobility of the profession. It can be beautiful to see.

Sensitivity, unaccompanied by strength, can so easily be trampled on. But such a daily exercise of strength before an external challenge can sometimes lead to hardening. There are many forms of 'toughness', a few of them eventually slip unnoticed into some rigidity and closure. Such a repeated mobilization of our whole system develops into a habit and before we know it we relate to all of life's challenges in this way.

It is useful to remember that the ultimate reason we need strength and courage is not to do with facing down the outside world at all.

What is our strength for?

The true purpose of our strength is to sustain our openness, our sensitivity and gentleness, our full aliveness, even in the most trying of circumstances.

Our strength is most wisely used when it first flows inwards, when it sustains the health of our own inner world. The true measure of our courage is not our ability to face conflict undeterred, but to maintain our open heartedness and connection, even when we are fearful. The very word 'courage' refers us to the heart, 'coeur' (French), suggesting that to live with courage is to live full hearted, despite all. To maintain the pulse of human tenderness at the core of our being, even when pressure, pain or sadness might close it down or harden us.

This is important if we want to teach in difficult circumstances, across the course of many years, or just if we want to stay open to living a full life. It is important also because when we stand before a new generation we are a powerful message about adult life, its possibilities and qualities. Whether we want to or not, we are answering some fundamental questions for them. Among those questions are: "What does it mean to grow up? What are the qualities of this adulthood, and what parts of us must we lose in this process? Will it cost us? And for what exact benefits? Is adulthood a less vital form of life?"

Most importantly, perhaps, are these questions: "Should I open to life or close? Should I risk love and be passionate or armour myself, exercise caution, shut down? Do I even get to choose at all? "

These questions concern our fundamental orientation to life. They may seem far from what teachers have been hired to do; far from the tasks, essay titles and cognitive challenges we agreed to provide in our job description. Far from equations and physics, design technology and punctuation. It is unlikely our students will ever be formally assessed or marked on what they have learned in answer to these questions although life will surely provide sufficient moments of testing.

Nonetheless, these questions are never far from us in the classroom: They are foundational. They are simply its environment. Despite the content of our curriculum and the rigour of our lesson plan, the primary and most powerful instruction we will ever offer is our own - often unnoticed - embodied and very personal answer to these questions of how to live.

What are we saying when we have stopped talking?

We answer these questions not primarily through words and conscious behaviour but through example and the unconscious habits and attitudes that form the hidden infrastructure to our teaching. Children listen intermittently to the words adults speak, but they consistently ingest and eventually reproduce our behaviour. They see us very well. They experience what we do, how we talk to them, how we handle difficulty. They see what portions of our self we reveal or hide and what we get excited about or dampen down. They do all this through their lived experience of our living presence.

Our curriculum leader enters our classroom with a request. They see the degree of confidence or fear, openness or closure in the shift of our shoulders, the rhythms of our eye contact, the dance of moving in and out of personal space. They learn this is how an adult lives in the presence of authority. A student acts out in the room yet again, and they see the calculations of accommodation and confrontation in the definition of our jaw, or the swallowing of our throat. They learn this is how an adult lives in the presence of conflict. We are speaking all the time to our children and students. It's just that most often our conscious mind tends not to be the part of us doing the speaking.

Our invitation.

We are the embodiment of what we are inviting them towards. The future we seek to build is built in our own image, and we might do well therefore to consider how attractive or desirable that image (and reality) is. If we stand before them shut down, exhausted, dispassionate, disengaged or coercive, we beckon or harass them into joining us in a future that shares such qualities. If our particular form of toughness means that our frown and irritations are mobilised so much more easily and powerfully than our laughter and inspiration, we say to them, 'this is what it means... to grow up'.

Yet if our kind of determination allows us to remain open-hearted, passionately curious, deeply committed and vibrant, we can invoke these qualities too. If we can smile broadly, laugh from our bellies, discuss our subject wide-eyed with wonder, if we can meet opposition and conflict skillfully, with confidence and calm empowerment we speak powerfully to the next generation about the ways in which it is possible to grow up today.

'Making the peace vivid'.

I am reminded of a story from the life of one of my own inspirations, the writer George Leonard. One afternoon he spent time talking to a group of fellow veterans about their experience of war. Whatever their views on the war itself, they all shared a common problem. The war represented a kind of peak experience for them. They had never quite felt so alive since returning from combat. On his bike journey home Leonard reflected that until we make our peace as vivid as our war, young men will continue to seek violent conflict as the nearest substitute experience they can find for this yearned for aliveness. By the time he had arrived at his destination he had invented The Samurai Game, an amazing, moving and peaceful immersion into a world of conflict, honour and meaning inspired by the Samurai.

This story suggests to us that we, who stand before children daily, also have a role to play in 'making the peace - or adulthood - more vivid'.

One of the reasons many children move but reluctantly towards real maturity is how grey, dull and narrow our adult lives sometimes appear to them, how burdened our shoulders, and joyless our routines. In truth they have hit upon something. It's worth asking: What are the definitions of maturity that we actually invite our children towards? When we are not talking, what are we saying to them through our own behaviour about adulthood? What examples are we placing before them? Is there any juice in our displayed maturity? Or does a dryness, a suppression of playfulness and impulse, a denial of the blood and flesh of tragedy, seem a precondition for joining the adult club? Is the shift to adulthood fundamentally about changing which end of a 'big moan' you are on, from being the recipient to being the deliverer?

As a result children may get older each year, but not necessarily more mature. Too many end up entering, not adulthood, but a twilight, hybrid state the therapist Robert Masters has called 'adultescence'. Here they become either increasingly empowered little egos, without any relationship to an unfolding wisdom or a larger grasp of what being in community means; or having hit school leaving age, they are abandoned to zigzag through the events and forces in their lives without the resources to fully understand what is going on.

Strong back, open front.

To be clear, I am not advocating teachers to be mere entertainers of children, desperately enticing them into maturity with a sparkly sense of yippee fun. Children are not fooled by such superficiality. And they will certainly not offer it their own depths. They are, however, fascinated both by joy and excitement. And by how human beings might live through tragedy and difficulty with nobility and grace. We mustn't collapse maturity down into pleasantness. Part of life is dangerous. And part of adulthood's allure should be that it remains mysterious, somewhere further away and beyond their ability to fully comprehend its shape.

I am advocating for our schools to encourage teachers to have lives that are visibly abundant, meaningful, inspired and challenging. For schools to support teachers more and for teachers to stand before children with a strong back and an open front, connected to and open about the richness of their lives, confident in their fundamental intelligence and strength, facing a difficult world with hope and determination and humour. I am advocating for teachers to embody great heart, and guts, as well as intellect.

Extract adapted from "Inspiring Presence:- Mindful teaching with heart and body."

(Forthcoming.)

The Embodied Rescue Dynamic - Nancy Shanteau

The Embodied Rescue Dynamic – Get Unstuck By Listening to Your Body, Asking for 100% of What You Want and Negotiating New Agreements.

I live in a sweet little jewel box of a house. Each room splashed with bright paint colors, art hung cheerily on walls, floral velvet curtains and geometric rugs – everything is creative and inviting. I had been living alone in the house for three years before my partner moved in with me after a few months of dating. While he wasn't particularly interested in renovating the interior design, he did want me to share the space – he was a painter and he liked to hang his artwork throughout the house. We made space for him on the walls and in the closets, bathroom, and living areas, but it seemed increasingly to be a problem for him that the house was so clearly "my space." Our aesthetic difficulties escalated over the couch. I'd spent two months selecting a vintage, tufted three-seater and getting it reupholstered in zebra velveteen. It was my pride and joy. He had a big golden retriever and in his life, dogs were welcome on couches. I didn't want him or the dog to feel unwelcome, nor did I want to give up my black and white couch.

We had reached a conundrum – a moment where our needs were directly opposed. If I relented and allowed the dog on the couch, it would get filthy, and I loved that couch. If the couch got dirty, I was afraid I would feel that sinking, nauseous feeling that I associated with anger and resentment. I worried that all my work and money on the couch would be lost when the couch was ruined after one winter with a long-haired dog. He wanted to feel "at home" and that he had a say in the arrangements of the house. He didn't want to feel heavy and stuck or get angry and resentful because I "always got my way."

This kind of argument shows up with couples in my office all the time. People live together and their genuine, dignified needs come into direct conflict. Often, when there is a scarcity of time, energy, resources, and space, people will end up either giving in or fighting to win. Neither approach is sustainable. A focus on winning and losing brings the energy of competition into a relationship, and we may end up feeling overwhelmed and exhausted from doing more than our share, or we might feel like a victim – hyper-vigilant and clenched or slack and resigned, hurt and angry that we lose our voice and our ability to make things happen. Our daily lives go so fast. We often work outside the home, and the culture tells us our homes and relationships should be sources of peace, love and support, not places of conflict and disagreement. When differences arise, decisions need to be made, and the work of sitting down and wrestling with opposing needs can seem daunting and hopeless.

The Embodied Rescue Dynamic in Relationships: A Tempting Shortcut

In Skills for Change coaching, we use the Embodied Rescue Dynamic to help us analyze what happened in the past and how to get unstuck so that we make agreements that work for everyone. The Rescue Dynamic theory comes from Eric Berne's Transactional Analysis and I first read about it in *Radical Therapy: The Second Decade*, edited by Beth Roy and Claude Steiner. Because we make change most effectively through the body, I help clients feel how the various energies of the rescue dynamic shape their bodies, and we design micro-interventions that help them make different choices moment by moment in the midst of difficult transactions. By paying attention to how power is used in a simple transaction, such as what to do about a zebra couch and a golden retriever dog, we can see where we are skipping important steps in our negotiations, and remind ourselves to re-center our bodies, words and actions around what we want to produce in our relationships and lives.

Let's consider the energies of the embodied rescue dynamic.

Rescue: We are *rescuing* when we do more than our share or more than we want to do. Often in people's bodies, *rescue* will show up as overextension – we lean forward, move faster and toward the other; there is often a lot of upper body action. The legs are involved as sources of energy and motion, although people who feel *rescuer* energy tend not to feel grounded. When we give for too long or too often, we end up *burning out*, feeling exhausted and depleted, and moving into the *victim* state.

Victim: The energy of *victim* most often includes some kind of collapse although this will look different when we allow ourselves to feel like a *victim* versus when we fight or avoid feeling this way. Most people will breathe shallowly and we might notice some kind of compression of the spine, sag in our shoulders, and dropping of our head and gaze. When we feel exhausted and overwhelmed by *victim* energy, we are unable or unwilling to do our share of the work. Some of us stay in the *victim* state for a long time, and may end up depressed and resigned, while others of us will attempt to avoid the *victim* state, *rebelling* and moving into the energy of *persecution* as a way to shift our shape and make a change.

Persecutor: In the energy of *persecutor*, people report feeling a range of emotions from slightly irritated to frustrated and impatient, increasing in intensity through anger and even rage. In the *persecutor* stage of the embodied rescue dynamic, we might identify our feelings and shape as appropriate for a "fight:" our muscles harden, our gaze narrows, we might take a wider stance in our feet and square our shoulders. We might feel righteous and certain we know what the other person did to cause us to feel this way. Once again, our energy tends to move up and forward, this time with more physical tension throughout our body. Some of us avoid these "negative" feelings and attempt to bypass the *persecutor* state, feel *guilty* for our "bad" *victim* and *rebellion* behavior and return to the *rescue* state. Others will explode in anger, and then feel *guilt* and shame for our outburst and attempt to repair through more *rescue*.

My partner and I were in the early stages of love and we were both *rescuing* – doing more than our share trying to solve the problem of the couch. He brought home a leather love seat from the thrift store and designated it the "dog couch." I found a set of blankets that I threw over the zebra couch to keep it clean for everyday use. I felt more and more resigned as the zebra couch got dirtier, and he reacted more defensively when I would sigh about the stains. But we didn't sit down and talk about each decision before we took action. We were tripping over ourselves trying to "fix it" and failing. The problem with shortcuts is that people don't have the same stories about what each other is doing and feeling and why. We tend to tell stories to ourselves where we are the central figure – we interpret the world through our own viewpoint, and our own values. Yet we don't really know what the other person is thinking and feeling unless we ask. My partner's and my body were growing more and more tense and I found myself avoiding the living room altogether. We both knew something was wrong but neither of us knew what to do about it.

I didn't like the "dog couch" – it was covered in a veneer of mud and dirt and seemed impossible to keep clean. Plus it made the living room feel crowded – my partner's solution to our space problems seemed to be "more furniture" and he didn't tend to ask me before he brought something home. When we *rescue*, we tend to *burnout*, and lose energy. Not only are we doing more than our share, often we don't get appreciated for our actions because the other person didn't ask us to do whatever we're doing. I started feeling like a *victim* in the department of house aesthetics – in order for him to feel powerful and that he had a "say," it seemed I had to agree to everything he wanted. As time passed, my sense of irritation and frustration grew. I was *rebelling* against my internal sense that I should "just go along and make things work" and moving into *persecutor* energy in the rescue dynamic. I felt myself tensing up every time the dogs jumped on a couch or shook themselves dry after coming in from the rain. See Illustration 1.

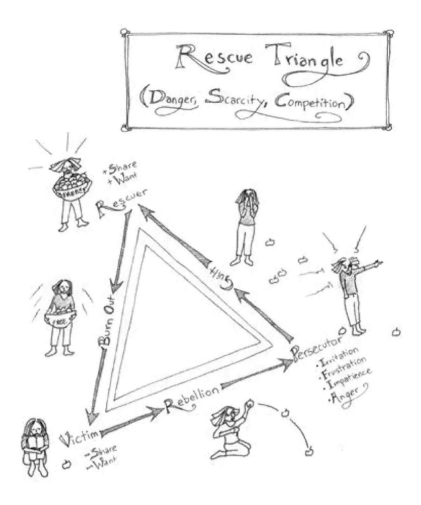

Rescue Triangle
(Danger, Scarcity, Competition)

Miranda Currie
Art and Illustration
www.mirandacurrie.com

NANCY SHANTEAU
COACHING
WWW.NANCYSHANTEAU.COM

I knew that if I got angry and said what I was thinking, we might end up fighting over the couch, the house, and how we were sharing power as a couple and I didn't want that. I also didn't want to keep *rescuing*. It was past time for me to figure out what I wanted and sit down for a conversation with my partner.

Ask for 100% of What You Want: Moving from Rescue to Cooperation

I sat down with a pen and paper and started writing down my needs. "I want to feel loved and connected. I love my house and I want the aesthetic to be beautiful, harmonious, clean and tidy. I want my partner and his dog to feel welcome. I want my zebra couch to stay clean and be presentable when we have guests. I want to feel happy and satisfied with our agreements. I want to feel relaxed and at ease. I want to have a say in every piece of furniture and make decisions about what stays and goes together." As I wrote the last sentence, I realized I wasn't telling myself the whole truth about what I wanted. I wanted my partner to love my house and aesthetic as much as I did, and I wanted him to let me make all the decisions. It sounded unreasonable, even in my head, so I'd suppressed my desire for control, and had gradually been feeling more and more unhappy about how the house looked. I had been overpowering myself internally because I didn't think I should want "control" – so instead I'd been giving into my partner's requests and changes without speaking up and asking for what I wanted. I'd been rescuing both internally and externally, and we weren't going to come to a resolution until I admitted what I wanted to myself and to him. No wonder I had felt so conflicted; internally I was all knotted up.

This kind of thing happens a lot. We have an idea of how to be "good" or "right" and we impose that behavior on ourselves without examining the cost or consequences. Yet, my desire for control of the aesthetics in the house wasn't "good" or "bad" – it just was. Until I asked him what he wanted, I wouldn't know how he felt about the house, the decorating style, or the furniture, and part of me was afraid to bring it up or ask because I might hear something I didn't like. He might want control also, or he might not care about the aesthetic, and might not agree on standards of tidiness, cleanliness or spaciousness. I was afraid to lose, so instead of asking for what I wanted, I had been collapsing, giving in, and feeling resigned. But it wasn't working. My irritation was becoming impatience with tinges of resentment, and I knew I was keeping secrets not just from him but also from myself. My tension was turning into a closed rigidity and I knew I was acting less loving and more remote. If I didn't share my feelings, I would continue drifting toward loss of love and disconnection.

Conversation and Cooperation: How Micro-Interventions Help Us Embody What We Want When We Negotiate Agreements

We invite clients to begin a negotiation by asking for 100% of what they want. Often, I see people do an internal calculus. "He wants to see an action film and I want to see a feel-good family movie. I'll suggest we go see a documentary I think we'd both be interested in seeing." Under these circumstances, we begin a negotiation asking for perhaps 70% of what we want, in hopes of getting it. In addition, our bodies reflect the embodied rescue dynamic – we are attempting to negotiate from desperation and our off-center, over-forward collapse or rigidity will produce confusing mixed messages that undermine our words. Often, our conversation partner doesn't know what we're thinking, but knows something isn't quite right. "I don't know about that documentary. I want to see the action film. I know you don't want to see it – how about that award-winning drama?" If I re-center, forgive myself for getting stuck in the rescue dynamic and ask if my partner wants to see the feel-good family movie, maybe he will just say yes. Or maybe, since we were trying to find a feel-good movie, he'll suggest a comedy. Our negotiation is much more likely to result in a happier course of action if we start from each person's relaxed, centered, whole and complete list of needs and wants.

I reminded myself that I wanted the relationship to work, and that my needs were dignified, even if I thought I "shouldn't" want control. I noticed I was clenching my jaw and my anal sphincter, and my stomach felt tight and agitated. I practiced speaking my 100% list of wants and needs out loud and noticed my voice felt forced and tight. I needed to change my shape if I wanted to invite my partner into a different agreement. If I approached him in this shape, I imagined he would interpret me as thinking I was "right" and he was "wrong" and we'd be worse off than if I said nothing. I like to help clients find tiny changes they can make in their physical body – something small they know they can do even when triggered. A micro-intervention might be as simple as opening our hands and resting them flat on our thighs, bending our knees or flexing our toes, settling our weight back into our heels, or opening and relaxing our jaw. I stay away from suggesting changes in the torso or breath – those tend to be easier after we've made changes in the peripheral muscles and limbs. For myself, I noticed my gaze was very narrowly focused. I raised my head and opened my peripheral vision. Automatically, I took a deep breath and relaxed my sphincter. My back body began to relax and open and I settled back in the chair. I wanted my partner to know that I was working hard on this topic because I loved him and I wanted to find a solution that worked for both of us. As my shape shifted, I knew I was more present, receptive and able to connect. In this relaxed body, I was more likely to speak in a way that he could hear, and also listen to him and what he wanted with an open mind and heart.

I asked my partner to prepare for a negotiation about the couch. He wrote, "I want the dogs to be comfortable. I want a place to sit that's clean and inviting and nice for cuddling. I want to be able to make decisions about the house and furniture without consulting you. I want both of us to keep the house clean and tidy. I want you to be happy about the couch and the house. I want you to tell me what's wrong instead of just sighing." After listening to his 100% and sharing mine, we considered the gaps in what we wanted. I wanted to make decisions about furniture and decorating together or by myself, and he wanted to make decisions by himself. After asking some questions, I discovered that he wanted me to participate in cleaning the house more often. I agreed to make a chore list and a schedule, and asked if he was going to buy furniture without consulting me, could I have a veto. He agreed. We decided to get rid of the dog couch and replace it with dog beds that took up less space and could be laundered. I agreed to let him know sooner when I was feeling uncomfortable. We planned to spend more time on the couch cuddling and less time watching television. We were both satisfied and happier with our new agreements and our relationship than we had been before we started.

Moving from Rescue to Cooperation - An Improbable Ideal

After I've taught clients the rescue dynamic, they often go home and try to eradicate rescue from their lives. When it doesn't work, and they continue to get triggered into old shapes and rescue patterns, they feel bad about themselves as if they've failed. In Skills for Change, we define a cooperative relationship as one where we agree to the following contract: no secrets, no lies, no rescues and no power plays. This contract represents an ideal – and in our fast and busy lives, it is difficult to implement fully. It takes time, effort, and determination to uproot rescue from our own embodied habits, and then further shift out of the rescue dynamic in the patterns we have with another person. Our awareness is important – first we notice when we're rescuing, do the best we can to figure out our 100%, re-center our bodies, then share our feelings, and ask for changes. But sometimes a relationship just isn't cooperative. We might be operating in a hierarchy where a leadership position demands we keep secrets from employees, or we might have a relationship where our differences in power make it extremely difficult to build the trust required for the other person to share their vulnerability.

Sometimes there are no non-rescue options. We have this fantasy in the culture that there's always a win/win solution available. What I've seen is that when our dignified needs are directly in competition with someone else, often we are faced with a choice between two rescues. After re-examining the possibilities and reassuring ourselves that really there are only rescue options available, I encourage clients to choose the "least worst rescue." When we make a choice, even when it's not a good choice, we can then make an agreement with ourselves to do the best we can and be compassionate with ourselves for contending with such a difficult dilemma. From that compassionate place we can re-center our bodies to act with the greatest power and grace possible under the circumstances.

Once I've taught clients the basics of the rescue dynamic, and they begin to see the patterns for themselves, we can do an advanced embodiment exercise that is very informative for the relationship. I'll invite one partner to get up and show us their embodied rescuer shape – I have them walk around the room and describe it for us along with the thoughts that go with it. Then I ask them to show us what happens when they start to burn out. We continue, acting out the embodied victim, persecutor, and guilt stages of the dynamic. Then we design micro-interventions for the moments throughout the dynamic where they are most likely to recognize they are stuck. After this thoughtful process, which is usually full of "a-ha moments" for both partners, we switch partners and do the process again with the second partner. These insights build understanding of how we embody the rescue dynamic and the micro-interventions provide us with ways to exit the rescue dynamic when we notice we are stuck.

In Conclusion – Acceptance, Compassion, and Action

Ultimately, my relationship with my partner ended. We couldn't solve the extreme differences in our needs by negotiating. Our fights got worse and he needed to get his way more and more often in order to feel like he had power in the relationship. When I asserted my boundaries, he decided to leave. His dog had puppies and one of them is sleeping next to me on the zebra couch as I write these words. There's a blanket on the couch to keep it mostly clean. Now instead of making new agreements with my partner, I navigate the differences between my needs and the needs of a sweet golden labrador. Life presents us with many twists and turns. We work to make changes in ourselves and our embodied habits and patterns, and sometimes it's not enough. Our needs are too different. Yet the work we put into understanding and communicating each other's needs is not wasted – we have greater acceptance of our vulnerability and limitations, and the maturity that comes with grief and loss.

The effort to shift the embodied rescue dynamic and change our ingrained behavior is worth it. When we understand how we rescue and attempt to bring our transactions into the open, re-center our bodies around what we want, negotiate, and make agreements that work for everyone, we deepen our connection with ourselves, increase the intimacy in our relationships, and build a community that offers mutual support. People discover creative solutions that while seeming extraordinarily unusual, allow both close connection and also meet competing needs. I've also been blessed to see people part ways with deep love and respect for each other. As a practitioner, the rescue dynamic offers clients relief – it explains what's happening and gives us hope there's something we can do to make things better. This awareness builds our adult consciousness – the internal space generated by our non-judgmental self-observation. Most of the positive life changes I help clients achieve emerge from this wise consciousness. It takes enormous self-love and confidence to tell ourselves the truth, share our vulnerability, accept the unacceptable, offer ourselves and each other compassion, re-center our bodies around our vision for the future, and then use our power to step forward and, even in the face of great loss, create the lives we want most.

Poetry - Beka Card

Becoming

The land inhabits me.

I'm like the porous membrane

of a single cell -

absorbing bird song,

lichen,

rock face

becoming

my genetic make-up.

I'm not here to live

half-heartedly.

I'm here to live on the edge

where Wild Mind

meets Wild Life.

I cannot tell where

my body begins, or ends.

This time, it carries with it

a quality of substance, of earth.

This time I haven't

disappeared – gone to dust

in jubilant escapism.

This time I'm here

whilst being It All.

One moment I'm a deer

taking precisely the medicine she needs

from the hedgerow.

The next moment

I'm the moss encasing the oak.

I'm not here to live within the confines

of the four walls -

I'll leave that for others.

Soon, I will dissolve completely

into the landscape.

You'll see my face in the beech bark,

Hear my voice in the

Blackbirds song

and the howling south-westerly.

The Shape of Shame - Clare Myatt

S h a m e. The word alone is enough to bring on a visceral response. (Never mind careless pronouncements like "shame on you", "what a shame", "you should be ashamed of yourself"). If, like me, you've grown up with shame as familiar as the nose on your face, perhaps you too are interested in a working definition of shame, how it feels, its etiology, how it shapes us, ways to modulate its grip and what happens if we do. This article aims a brief exploration of the landscape and invites your own musings.

By definition, shame is something we don't want to talk about. We have a natural tendency to avoid things that make us squirm and feel uncomfortable. A brave researcher brought shame into the mainstream in 2010 with an internet hit on the healthy counter-point to shame - vulnerability. Her name is Dr. Brene Brown and her original talk on TED.com[1] has over sixteen million hits. Her subsequent 2012 TED talk[2] on listening to shame has over four million. She describes

---

[1] https://www.ted.com/talks/brene_brown_on_vulnerability

shame as the "unspoken epidemic"[3] of our time. What I don't hear about is the shape of shame. How is it embodied? Plenty of insightful information about its origin, development, impact, consequences....but very little about its embodiment. As a somatic specialist this seems to be a big gap in our understanding and this is what I'm interested in exploring.

I have a particular interest here, a deeply personal one. With twenty-five years recovery from alcoholism under my belt, I had anticipated being pretty much done with shame by now, but shame remains. And it gets in the way of things I want to do and achieve. (Writing, would you believe, is one of those things). In addition, I specialise in the treatment of trauma and addiction from a somatic perspective and am constantly reminded of the confluence of shame, trauma and addiction, blending like the ingredients in a cake, becoming inseparable. I support my clients in their healing journey, appreciate seeing them blossom, but then see limitations due to the underlying grip of shame. For some the limitations will be in the domain of

---

[2] http://www.ted.com/talks/brene_brown_listening_to_shame

[3] http://www.ted.com/talks/brene_brown_listening_to_shame

intimacy and connection, for others perfectionism and being driven to perform, yet others will be confounded by self-expression and creativity.

A working definition

Let's begin with the distinction between guilt and shame. Guilt relates to how I feel when I've done something which goes against accepted social mores. It's a "doing" fault[4]. Shame relates to something intrinsically wrong or bad about me. Instead of "I've done something bad" the shame-based person says "I am bad." It's a "being" fault.[5] And just to complicate matters, it's possible to feel both guilt and shame. For example, if I take a train journey without buying a ticket I

---

[4] For a rigorous exploration of shame, especially as it relates to alcoholism, addiction and the twelve steps of Alcoholics Anonymous, see Ernest Kurtz "Shame and Guilt" 2007 http://www.hindsfoot.org/eksg.html

[5] Ernest Kurtz "Shame and Guilt" 2007 http://www.hindsfoot.org/eksg.html

feel guilty; if that goes against my personal standards of integrity and honesty I feel ashamed. I've done something bad and I am bad.

On a related level, what does shame feel like? Kurtz says if guilt is a "pang" then shame is an "ache"[6]. It permeates, perhaps alleviated for a while in the face of success, satisfaction, happiness, then returns. Sometimes there is a deep wash of it, something I call a shame spiral as it seems to have that effect on me - keeps going around and around, intensity varying, always heat, then ultimately dying away, leaving me feeling warm, uncomfortable and looking for an exit.

Etiology of shame

So, why do some people develop only guilty pangs from time to time, others develop a tolerable level of shame, the kind that seems to be a necessary part of the human condition, yet others develop a full-blown shame-based existence, informing their very being? Without

---

[6] Ernest Kurtz "Shame and Guilt" 2007 http://www.hindsfoot.org/eksg.html

taking a long detour into resilience and personal resources, which seem to influence one's ability to tolerate trauma and shame, we believe that shame develops in response to one or more significant events that are traumatic in nature. And by traumatic, I mean an event occurring somewhere on the continuum between small 't' trauma and capital "T" Trauma. (Small "t" trauma at one end of the continuum is falling off a bike and being laughed at; capital "T" trauma at the other end of the continuum is the unspeakably horrific, humiliating prisoner-of-war torture we don't want to believe humans are capable of).

Rather than experience the helplessness, powerlessness, potentially overwhelming hopelessness of such a traumatic event, we scab over the wound with shame. We feel shame instead of something akin to death, being slightly more palatable. We take the blame (where none is justified) and feel inherently bad. Not just that a bad thing happened (although it most likely did) but that fundamentally we are flawed, bad and wrong.

Here's a further distinction, from Staci Haines: "shame emerges as an automatic response to a tear in the fabric of trust."[7] The "fabric of trust" distinction is important for it reveals the part played by relationship. Trust is broken in relationship and, by definition, can only be healed in the context of relationship. Much as we may want to heal alone, away from the eyes of another, the work has to be done in context of relationship. Often a therapeutic one, where (hopefully) the relationship is real yet professional and contained to provide the optimal environment for healing. Now, this is difficult and courageous terrain. It's been my experience as client that my internal dialogue goes something like this: "geez, you want me to reveal my innermost secrets, the kind that make me squirm, tell you all about them and believe you't not going to judge me? Yeah, right." As practitioner, it helps to understand this deeply, enabling me to be present and provide an accepting, warm environment.

As you can see, the spiral of trauma and shame is the near perfect breeding ground for self-medication to ease the pain. Whether it be through mood or mind-altering substances (alcohol and other drugs, nicotine, food, etc.) or behaviours (gambling, sex, shopping, etc.), there is relief from the misery of self-loathing shame brings - at least

for a while. In my experience, trauma doesn't always lead to addiction,

[7] Haines, S. Somatics and Trauma training; 2004. San Francisco

but it often does. And this brings me full-circle to the shape of shame. What does it look like?

Shape of shame

I've found little about the shape of shame in the literature. A thorough, but admittedly not exhaustive, search has revealed the following. Alexander Lowen, M.D., the founder of Bioenergetics, describes how we hide our face in shame[8]; Richard Strozzi-Heckler, Ph.D., describes a client who "walked the path of somatically unwinding the shame and pain of the trauma and committed to new practices that built her resilience and new shape."[9] Staci Haines refers to shame throughout her book[10], yet little is offered about the

[8] http://fullpermissionliving.blogspot.co.uk/2009/05/body-language-by-alexander-lowen.html

[9] p.129 The Art of Somatic Coaching, see Bibliography

[10] Haines, Staci. Healing Sex: A Mind-Body Approach to Healing Sexual Trauma. Cleiss Press, 2007

physical shape. Even Stanley Keleman, in his seminal book Emotional Anatomy[11] doesn't talk directly about the shape of shame, although it is often alluded to.

The most useful is a rather dense article published in 2003 by Thomas Fuchs entitled The Phenomenology of Shame, Guilt and the Body in Body Dysmorphic Disorder and Depression[12] wherein he states:

"...the characteristic experience of shame itself: being painfully affected by centripetal directions, i.e., by piercing gazes or pointing fingers from all sides; lowering one's eyes in order to escape those gazes; a feeling of shrinking such as one could "sink through the floor with shame," a desperate desire to hide oneself—all this means paralysis and corporealization in the presence of the others. The reddening and warmth of the face, or the "burning shame" corresponds to the painful gazes which are felt like hot rays; the ashamed person is actually the "focus" of attention. This

---

[11] Keleman, Ph.D., S. Emotional Anatomy. Center Press, 1989

[12] https://www.klinikum.uni-heidelberg.de/fileadmin/zpm/psychatrie/fuchs/Shame.pdf

phenomenological structure of shame means that the lived-body has taken up and internalized its being seen; the exposure as corporeal body before the eyes of the others has become a part of its feelings. Thus we may say that shame is the incorporated gaze of the other."

Beyond the theoretical, the popularity of both Brene Brown's TED talks and her books[13] suggest a conventional wisdom exists - ask most people and they can visualise someone shame-based, can demonstrate what they look like, how they stand, or even show how they personally experience shame. I know I can. Can you?

Even in writing this, I find myself sagging a little. My breastbone dips, collapsing ever so slightly. The more I contemplate shame the more my chest begins to cave in, collapsing, pulling down and away. Breath is harder, my lungs don't fill effortlessly, a tiny crease begins in that place between my eyebrows, one shoulder starts its natural climb toward my ear, and my heart begins to beat a tiny bit faster. It's the antithesis of filling up my chest with honour and pride, not in an arrogant way, but a self-accepting "hmmm, did well there" type way.

---

[13] The Gifts of Imperfection and Daring Greatly, see Bibliography

Is this the shape? Is it the same for everyone?

Based on self and other observation, I think there may be an inner shape and a corresponding similar, or dissimilar, outer shape. For example, someone with a corresponding similar inner and outer shape has this kind of look: eyes dropped or averted; jaw and mouth area most likely tense and constricted; head tipped forward reflecting the desire to disconnect and look away; shoulders anywhere from slightly rounded to slumped forward, on that continuum from slight uh-oh to helpless; breast-bone sagging downwards, collapsing backwards toward the spine; resultant constriction through the diaphragm impedes deep breaths which are shallow, either fast or slow depending on other factors; from the solar plexus down, little energy apparent, it's as if they have no legs - they could be thrown off balance without warning, don't know how to recover from that, and there's an absence of sensation reflecting a lack of connection to the past because it's too hard to bear, and a lack of connection to the future because there's little hope.

Comparatively, there are those who have this kind of inner landscape yet their outer presentation is dissimilar. They have a counter way of being in the world, compensating for this internal collapse. Head may be high with chin thrust forward, eyes able to make contact then dart away; shoulders and chest braced as if ready to defend, probably hard or unyielding to the touch; bracing creates little room for the breath so diaphragm moves minimally and solar plexus is somehow protected by being pulled in. From the solar plexus down, there may be more presence in the pelvis and legs, but that presence is connected to protection and defense rather than creativity or owning history. We could say the outside is strong, the inside is scared, fuelled by internalised shame.

Modulating the grip of shame

All this makes me wonder whether there is a somatic component to recovering from shame. (Which, in turn, has considerable consequences for recovery from addiction and trauma). My training and experience tells me yes there is. It is possible to develop an embodied way of being to alleviate the hold shame can have, allowing us to become more whole. Opening up the doors to what Brene Brown calls "the gifts of imperfection."[14]   Here we find self-acceptance, satisfaction, fulfilment, gratitude, happiness.....surely, everything most people strive for?

Perhaps the best way to explore the possibility is to experiment. As best you can, try this:

* Imagine, visualise or recall a time when you felt shame. Perhaps this is recent, perhaps this is long ago. Try to choose something that scores a one or two out of ten on the scale of severity rather than a full-blown eight or nine out of ten. We want to play with something that isn't going to pitch you into a spiral difficult to recover from. Pay close attention to what's happening in your body, particularly sensation and change in shape and posture. What do you notice? What's happening? Has your temperature changed? Do you have any impulses? Is there more stillness or more movement?

Now shake that out. Stretch, move, walk around, have a drink of water, shift the mood and the body. Next, do this:

* ~~Imagine, visualise or recall a time when you felt proud or happy,~~
14   The Gifts of Imperfection, see Bibliography

settled, full, satisfied. Perhaps this is recent, perhaps this is long ago. It could be a tender moment with someone you care about; walking in the wonder of nature and smelling the scent of newly cut grass, or lavender, or roses; feeling satisfied when you finished a book or a project, a journey or a task; celebrating something you enjoyed doing either alone or with others....whatever has you feel clear, positive, hopeful, satisfied. Pay close attention to what's happening in your body, just like you did before, particularly sensation and change in shape and posture. What do you notice? What's happening? Has your temperature changed? Do you have any impulses? Is there more stillness or more movement?

The Outcome

I wonder what you've noticed? I can tell you what I've noticed for myself, and what I've observed in others. Having already described what I believe to be the shape of shame, I'll focus on the counter. In one word, I feel empowered. Just a little bit taller, wider, deeper, somehow more substantial. Fully in my body and settled there. Neither too warm nor cool, my temperature feels just right. Sensation is soft and gentle, more in the background than foreground, a sense of calm and stillness although I know I could move if I wanted to, I'm not immobilised. The negative voices in my head quieten down and may silence altogether. My chest feels open, maybe even a little vulnerable, but in a good way, having a sense of being able to connect deeply with others from this tender place. I have the sense this is a place which can produce intimacy. I feel satisfied and hopeful, that more is possible than I thought before.

So, how did I produce this? I've been practicing something I learned at Strozzi Institute[15] many years ago called grounding and centering[16], enhancing and fine-tuning the process over time. Many of you reading this, interested in embodiment, will already know how to get grounded in the body. Briefly, this is the process:

> Stand with feet hip distance apart and breathe a little more deeply

> Feel your feet engaged with the earth

---

[15] www.strozziinstitute.com

[16] p. 89 Anatomy of Change: A Way to Move Through Life's Transitions, see Bibliography

> Relax the knees, buttocks, belly, pelvic floor, shoulders, jaw and eyes

> Drop the attention to the belly (the hara or tan tiens)

> Then center along length (for dignity), width (your social presence) and depth (for gravitas) [17]

For those who haven't practiced grounding and centering before, there may not be a sense of wellbeing the first time, this is one of those "simple not easy" practices that builds in reward over time. What I can promise you is that practiced repetitively, over time, this will shift your physical and emotional state. And while I have no empirical evidence, I have anecdotal feedback that this practice makes a significant difference to one's sense of wellbeing and empowerment. That being said, on the basis practice makes permanent, I invite you to begin the three hundred repetitions it takes to get this into muscle memory (three thousand for embodiment)[18]

---

[17] If you would like a three minute audio guide to this process, please contact me via my website, see the contributor listing at the front of the Journal

[18] per Richard Strozzi-Heckler, Ph.D. quoting US military research

Conclusion

In defining shame and its etiology, revealing its relationship to trauma and addiction, initial thoughts about the shape of shame in the body have been proposed and explored. I have no empirical data on which to draw, just deep curiosity and observation about myself and others, backed up with some anecdotal feedback from clients and colleagues with whom I'm engaged in ongoing conversation. Are you interested in contributing, becoming part of the conversation? If so, please email me: clare@claremyatt.co.uk. Together, let's generate something to make a difference to the millions of people dogged by shame; let's uncover the shape of shame and thereby the means for recovery from its grip.[19]

Bibliography

Brown, Ph.D., B. The Gifts of Imperfection: Let Go of Who You Think You're Supposed to be an Embrace Who You are. Hazelden, 2010

---

[19] A further article with what's generated will follow, so watch this space

Brown, Ph.D., B. Daring Greatly: How the Courage to Be Vulnerable Transforms the Way We Live, Love, Parent and Lead. Portfolio Penguin, 2013

Haines, Staci. Healing Sex: A Mind-Body Approach to Healing Sexual Trauma. Cleiss Press, 2007

Keleman, Ph.D., S. Emotional Anatomy. Center Press, 1989

Potter-Efron, Ph.D., R. Shame, Guilt and Alcoholism: Treatment Issues in Clinical Practice. Routledge, 2002

Strozzi-Heckler, Ph.D., R. Anatomy of Change: A Way to Move Through Life's Transitions. North Atlantic Books, 1997

Strozzi-Heckler, Ph.D., R. The Art of Somatic Coaching: Embodying Skillful Action, Wisdom and Compassion. North Atlantic Books, 2014

Creativity and Embodiment - Tess Howell

I've been looking at the links between art and embodiment. Why does creativity matter? Why would being centered in our core make a difference?

In this article I'm using "art" to mean the act of creating, whatever that creative outpouring looks like to us - perhaps painting, practicing the piano or playing with clay; maybe making a beautiful home space or building a bench - there is some kind of self-expression that comes through. We can distinguish between art therapy, art based coaching and art for arts sake - all three will show up here.

When I speak of embodiment I'm talking about a physical activity that consciously cultivates an aspect of the way that we move through the world. Intrinsic in the word 'cultivates' is an awareness of how it currently is and an aspiration of how it could be.

Aren't these both just middle class luxuries – some sort of happy hobby of artistic expression or a self-improvement drive related to the body beautiful? For me, no. Both are critical to living an awake and aware life. At the very minimum this means minimizing harm: living with some notion of self-care, concern for others and an awareness of the wider world. Our lives do matter, however peculiar and puzzling they may seem to us. We do have the chance to make an impact. At its very best being embodied, self expressed and present in our lives means we have some possibility of cultivating our passions and living our potential.

It sounds somewhat cliché, but our lives are our canvas - the way we move is who we are, it is our way of working in the world, our lives are our own design, whether we are conscious of it or not. This is an area where creativity and embodiment strongly intersect - we do literally create a life for ourselves and a specific stance on life- according to our field of focus and what we choose to cultivate.

In both modalities there can be a distinction between the polarities of working with cultivation and catharsis.

When we look at cultivation we can consider both embodiment practices and art based coaching. Art based coaching works with the "rehearsal of the possible", to try things out in the relative safety of the blank page and see how they feel, before we try them out in the outside world. Basic embodiment work sets us up with a similar enquiry - how would it be to move through life in a different way? Perhaps a little softer? Or perhaps with a little more fierce focus?

The techniques in art based coaching work don't tend to actively go "digging in the depths" in the way that conventional therapy does. We are not looking to work with our story. What happened, by whom and when may not be the most empowering questions we can ask. Certainly self-knowledge is important. Yet also asking what we want to do about it, now we know that that is how it is, may be a question that will serve us substantially more. Art based coaching works with those unconscious blocks, questioning what stops us from being where we want to be and how can we make better choices.

Embodiment links to leadership in this question of how do we lead change effectively. Time and time again it seems to be not just about what we are doing- it's who we are being. With this knowledge we can choose to cultivate what we embody. There are a thousand ways of being embodied - any physical practice can be utilised as a technique for increased embodiment to cultivate a particular quality of being –

it's just a case of being clear in advance what that aspect is. Knowledge really is power and self-awareness is important.

Embodiment practices allow us to be informed by all our ways of sensing:

When we are centered in our body we are open to the sensory input from our surroundings. We are not blocking life. We are receptive to what is really going on around us, minimizing denial, defiance and defence. We could be described as available to others, to ourselves, to life. It also helps us sustain our pace - body listening certainly helps us avoid burnout. Being embodied let's us show up more and more, in a sustainable way, for whatever work we are doing in the world.

Then there is the catharsis end of the spectrum - and I use the term very loosely here - to look at letting go of what doesn't serve us: of those habitually held tendencies that hinder us. Within art therapy the art work acts as a container, for all those things that could be felt or spoken as we are reclaiming some part of ourselves. A supportive space to let us re-member- in the literal sense of the word - to let life back in our limbs - where we may have become stifled or shut down. In terms of pure physiology, we build up stress and then discharge.

Trauma can be held in the body and there are a variety of physical practices that can help with the process of release. Our movement habits build momentum: after 20 or 30 years of stooping forwards over a keyboard it can then really take something significant to wake us up and make us uncurl, stretch out towards the sky. Art therapy works with the same principles - creating images on a page to express an aspect of the inner world that may not be available to memory or easy to articulate. People often come to therapy because something isn't working in an area of their lives - a space on the blank page is an excellent place to start the listening process as to what that something might be, and how we might enable its release.

For many the creative urge to "work things through" via art can be viewed as an imperative. Let's face it, for most folks it's a thoroughly inefficient way to earn a living; yet this urge to self-express and to communicate the intricacies of our inner worlds though a creative outlet has been cranking through us for centuries.

It is often useful to consider balance in seeking to consciously make a shift in a particular area of one's personal or professional lives. In both modalities there needs to be a balance of active and receptive. If we are excessively driven by action, a perpetual desire to be doing more, every minute of every day, then there is little space to hear that next creative impulse or bit of body listening arrive.

In both modalities, art coaching and embodiment, we are looking to listen to something else alongside the mind. Being receptive to a new idea or inspiration coming in when we need it most. Ever tried dancing, running stretching for twenty minutes and then getting to the page/canvas/keyboard? Trust me - the "muse" is appreciatively more audible after we have allowed ourselves some time to listen within these limbs.

What is the embodiment of creativity? It's a combination of being skilled enough in a particular medium that we have developed some aptitude at expressing something through it (i.e. a level of expertise) - and it also requires receptivity - to an idea, to the progression of a project. Many of the great creatives report that their work seems to flow through them, yet some serious study and a substantial knowledge-base is important here: a great deal of muscle memory is involved in mastery. In those early years when we are thinking about our learning, it uses up so much more mental capacity than when we can just embody an art-form such as piano-playing or painting. It is paradoxically when we stop concentrating intense effort on "learning it" and relax into really "being with it," that there is more space for that still, small voice of intuition to come in. This intersection of intuition plus informed experience is important in both awesome artwork and in effective and inspired embodied action.

Intuition should be given sufficient space of its own here too - embodiment teaches us to "trust our gut" those physiological pathways that guide us as we interact with others. The tightening of jaw or tension in the shoulders when we think of a particular course of action in our professional or personal lives may well guide us to look at our choices carefully. As may that angry squiggle and the underlined words pressed through the page when we jot down our feelings about two different courses of action. We would be well advised to notice these signals - they will likely serve us well.

We are not looking to bypass thorough thought, just to strengthen the links between the body and the brain, the information system between our intellect and our intuition.

Ultimately both modalities can be used to cultivate choice. Instead of moving through life on autopilot - how would it be to really know and notice what we are doing, the energy it takes and the effect it has.

We are, after all, social creatures: life on this plenty-filled but still fully finite planet goes a whole lot better when we show up and serve each other rather than getting lost in the tense shoulders, tight belly, tiny field of vision that accompanies the small seeing mind's mantra of more for me, more for me....

Really we are looking at increasing response-ability, the ability to respond to a situation, not just react in ways driven by our habitual tendencies and patterns. To be cultivating enough behavioural range, plus access to our own awareness, that we can make a consistently conscious choice.

I can't help but conclude that the link I am exploring here is presence. Both working with the body and being in our creative process are potent ways to land us right in the present moment, into that felt sense of flow.

We can see what we want to shift, how we might move differently and what kind of culture we want to be creating around us.

Ultimately we are looking at practices that provide us with effective ways of being mindful of what really matters most. Being body based, self-expressed and showing up; letting us move towards more moments of a life that we love.

Chronic Pain - an Embodiment? - Charlie Birch

From the first time I experienced back pain until the day I found the treatment approach that worked for me, I lived 10 years of my youth in chronic pain and said goodbye to my childhood dream of becoming a professional dancer. Today, I have been pain free for six years and use what I learned over the past 16 years to help other humans live pain free vital lives. In as little as 6 months, my holistic and integrative approach allows my clients to get the results they are seeking.

I have 23 years of experience with embodied practice. In this time I have noticed that the word 'embodiment' gets tossed around and used in all sorts of different ways. Oftentimes, embodiment professionals brush this off and dive into the 'work.' After all, language is an aspect of the mind and embodiment is about the body, right? Wrong! I believe that words have a significant impact on our experiences in our bodies. I also believe that words shape our values, our beliefs, and our paradigms, which we then express in part via our embodiment/s. I propose that words are a vital aspect of embodied work. Further, I believe the embodiment field is in great need of clear operational definitions and language. That is of course, if we want to make our work accessible and support people in embracing the vast wisdom and value this field has to offer.

Here I offer you some basic definitions, so you understand EXACTLY what I mean. Along the way, I will explain how these definitions inform my work with chronic pain. The end result being: a new mind-set about what causes pain to become chronic and what is possible in regards to healing.

Embodiment - a way of being in the world that is made up of an internal state and an external expression.

Chronic pain is one type of embodiment. In my personal and professional experience the internal state is an identity crisis. While the external expression is a super rigid identity that has been learned. In other words, the embodiment is one of stressful confusion, a general experience of who we *think* we are not lining up with who we *feel* we are. This embodiment is problematic, because it is not built on a foundation of integration. If you had asked me to describe myself 10 years ago, I would have told you... I love my family. I am easy going. I love to help people. I love dance. I love my friends... everything in my life is great, expect my damn back!

Embodied- a *felt sense* experience of residing in one's body.

People with chronic pain, are often preoccupied with their bodies and have very little awareness of what is going on in the mind; *thoughts and emotions.* They are in fact by default very embodied humans, because they spend most of their time attending to their experience of being in their bodies. I often suggest that these humans are actually stuck in their bodies. They simply experience their embodiment, but have not yet learned to influence and shift embodiments at will. They are not consciously embodying.

Embodying - taking on the qualities or characteristics of a being, place, energy, thing, etc.

Chronic pain is a way protecting ourselves emotionally from thoughts, feelings, and parts of ourselves that make us uncomfortable. When we have internal experiences that are deemed taboo by the subconscious and unconscious levels of the mind, pain is created. When the body is screaming out in pain there is very little room for other thoughts, ideas, and emotions to surface. The pain itself is often embodying a part of yourself, thoughts, emotions, shadow aspects, that do not have full permission around expression. Expression is the process of sequencing thoughts, ideas, and emotions from the inside out into the world. Thoughts, ideas, and emotions are forms of energy, so when we don't express them we have to repress them. Repression is the process of forcing energy to stay in the body and it requires a lot of effort. Embodying repression often results in a tense, rigid, and exhausting embodiment. The longer and more chronic this embodiment becomes, the more likely it is to cause physical pain. Teaching people to increase their embodiment capacities, empowers them to consciously reduce the frequency and severity of their pain.

Embodiment Practice - a mindfulness practice that engages the body and overtime allows an individual to cultivate a new quality or characteristic. A way of increasing the range and depth of individual's embodiment.

I use embodiment practices to help my clients gain comfort in expanding the range and depth of their embodiment capacities. So that they can stop repressing what they don't want and start expressing what they do want. This brings me back to my point on language. The way that each person explains and names their experience of chronic pain embodiment, provides personalized clues for how to help them shift. If someone says I feel rigid, I will prescribe them a practice that cultivates flexibility. If someone feels stuck, we work with freedom and flow. If someone feels like they are at war with themselves, we will work with harmony. In the most simple form I invite my clients to embody health, vitality, and functional integration.

Human System - the *entirety and interplay* between a person's mind body, physical body, and spirit body energies.

We are human systems. It is commonly accepted that humans have minds, bodies, and spirits. A system is made up of divergent parts converging to make a whole new thing. A living system is unique in that it is self correcting. No one can deny that we are living systems. It is commonly understood that the mind, body and spirit are separate. They are. However, they are equally, masterfully, and endlessly intertwined. If they weren't YOU would not be, because YOU are the result of these divergent parts self correcting to make a whole new thing. Embodiment work is not in service of your body, it is in service of you having more control over your life! Pain is not a body problem, it is a system malfunction that manifests in the physical self. Embodiment practice in service of healing chronic pain, is about giving people one of the toolboxes they need to self correct more consciously. It is also important to look at the rest of the system, so I ask what is the embodiment, what is the mindset, what is the spiritual perspective and how is that converging to produce a human system state.

Human System State - the *felt* sense of one's own system at any given moment in time.

As I said before I have an integrative and holistic approach. Embodiment is just one of the areas I am trained in. My other dominant influences include mindset, and spirituality. Ultimately for me, chronic pain is actually a system state. It has an embodiment, a mindset, and spiritual perspective. I support my clients in expanding their awareness of the problem, chronic physical pain, to include the mindset and the spiritual perspective. This makes it much easier to identify the variables involved in the creation and continuation of the symptoms, the recovery toolbox gets bigger, and the healing potential sky-rockets.

MindBodySpirit Integration - a system state where the 3 bodies (mind body, physical body, spirit body) are congruent and working together to create a functional whole.

My yoga teacher used to say yoga is a practice not a perfect. Life is the same, it's a practice not a perfect. I do help my clients heal and live pain free lives, but that is just the beginning. Embodiment is a huge part of what I do, but ultimately I teach MindBodySpirit Integration. So, just as embodiment is a type of practice, MindBodySpirit integration is a school of practice. Healing pain is just the beginning. Next comes growth and transformation.

Applications of Embodiment in Organisations

Benefits to Leadership, Communication, and Innovation - Anouk Brack

The maturing field of embodiment in the workplace

Embodiment in organisations has been developing for over 4 decades

Businesses not yet implementing embodiment in their Human Resource Development Policy might find themselves lagging behind in the coming years. The early adopters have been "on" it for decades already, seeing its continued use and aiding in its continued development. Some examples of the many businesses and organisations that have benefited from implementing embodiment work are: NASA, Hewlett Packard, Oracle, McKinsey, AFM (Dutch Authority for the Financial Markets), NHS (National Health Services, UK), CSA (Coaching Supervision Academy), NTR (Dutch Broadcast Agency), BBC (British Broadcast Corporation), WUR (Wageningen University and Research centre). There are many more.

Embodiment has its roots in the human potential movement

The seeds of embodiment as a useful method for human development were planted some decades ago in the sixties and seventies in the human potential movement (HPM) in California in the USA.[1] A few well-known proponents of that movement are George Leonard, Michael Murphy, and Jean Houston. Examples of teachers and writers responsible for subsequently shaping the field of embodiment are Wendy Palmer[2], George Leonard, Richard Strozzi-Heckler[3] and Paul Linden[4].

Two trends show embodiment entering mainstream business now

After a gestation period of a couple of decades of testing and improving, the time seems ripe now for it to come to fruition in the main stream. Two trends are supporting this claim: firstly, the immense rise in popularity of mindfulness practice as a stress reduction method. Mindfulness and embodiment are intimately linked as both have their roots in meditative practices and teach people to be more aware of the present moment. In order to cultivate mindfulness you practice proper body posture, breath and focus. Embodiment starts with mindfulness of the body-mind system and could also be seen as mindfulness in action. Secondly, the recent findings in neuroscience and embodied cognition support the ancient wisdom techniques (like martial arts principles) that embodiment is rooted in. More evidence for this will be presented in the science of embodiment section of this article.

Variety of applications of embodiment in organisations

In the past decades the amount of organisations implementing embodiment as a way to increase employee efficiency and health has been gradually increasing. The growth seems to be speeding up and its potential is impressive. Some of the variety of useful applications of embodiment in organisations are:

- Leadership Presence development

- Effective communication in challenging situations (like bad news conversations, presentations, difficult people)

- Stress reduction and burn out prevention

- Conflict resolution

- Decision making

- Team-building and team communication improvement

- Assertiveness, authenticity, intuition, innovation and creativity boost

– and many more

Embodiment is even valuable in combination with organisational development according to expert Martin Saville: "My experience is that offering appropriately designed Leadership Embodiment work with the (senior) management as part of a wider Organisation Development initiative can help people move more effectively through a process of change."[5] It helps the leadership to "walk the talk" so to speak, and that has a big influence on the involvement and commitment of the workforce to contribute to the goals of the operation."

Sharing these other-than-usual types of encounters with one another increases trust, openness, and understanding. This can lead to valuable team and relationship building even when the topic of the training is focused elsewhere.   Embodiment work can make communication more effective and team targets easier to reach.

The science behind the added value of embodied leadership

There is a growing evidence-base for embodied training[6]. Let's now take a look at research investigating the biological basis of effective leadership.

Combining power and connection optimizes leadership performance

Power posing expert Amy Cuddy (2013) beautifully summarizes the implications of these findings on neuroscience of embodiment for effective leadership in the article "Connect, then lead":

"A growing body of research suggests that the way to influence—and to lead—is to begin with warmth. Warmth is the conduit of influence: It facilitates trust and the communication and absorption of ideas. Even a few small nonverbal signals—a nod, a smile, an open gesture—can show people that you're pleased to be in their company and attentive to their concerns."

Stress-induced "amygdala hijacks" by our reptilian brain

The above may seem like common-sense to many of us but as the old saying goes "Just because it's common-sense doesn't mean it's common practice." Under pressure we are even more likely to forget even the most basic things. For optimal performance our physiological and psychological state is very important. If we are too stressed or reactive, our neocortex, the part of our brain capable of creative thinking, positive risk-taking and self-reflection goes "off-line". We suffer from what is called an amygdala hijack in which a lower part of our brain, also called reptilian brain, takes over for our safety.[15] In this state we are ego-centric and not able to give others a sense of connection. The well-known survival patterns fight, flight, and freeze kick in: stage fright and forgetting your point when the CEO suddenly turns his attention on you is an example of freezing. Your angry defensiveness when challenged in a meeting is a fight response. This is an unconscious and involuntary process. Our higher functions are often still aware, giving us an excruciatingly frustrating experience where we are aware of what we're doing, but we can't stop it.

Conquering amygdala hijack

Here we find one of the greatest benefits of applying embodiment in organisations. We can learn to recognise, prevent and recover from an amygdala hijack. Because the higher brain functions are often powerless our best chance for learning to recover is using embodiment practices where we shift our state in the body and allow this to influence brain function. During the hijack we can use deep breathing, focussed muscle relaxation, and a rehearsed statement to self about the bigger picture. In Leadership Embodiment "centering" is the basic practice for achieving exactly this.[16] When we are centered, we can offer the best of ourselves to the situation and make a bigger contribution.

[Editor's Note: Clare Myatt describes the process of centring in her article]

To reduce the chances of getting off-centre, self-care in all its forms will help us—exercise, diet, relaxation, meditation. Mindfulness practice can help to raise the threshold of the amygdala hijack, thereby increasing the chances of functioning optimally more of the time.[17]

Powerful poses enhance performance

Amy Cuddy who I quoted at the beginning of this section on the science supporting the value of embodiment has a famous piece of research which she speaks about in a TED talk. She found that standing or sitting in a powerful pose for two minutes influences hormone levels in the bloodstream subsequently influencing the way we feel and our performance[7] for instance in a job interview. "High power posers performed better and were more likely to be chosen for hire"[8] due to their presentation quality (e.g., captivating, confident).

Testosterone plays a role in both men and women and is known to reduce fear in humans.[9] "High-power posers experienced elevations in testosterone, decreases in cortisol, and increased feelings of power and tolerance for risk; low-power posers exhibited the opposite pattern."[10]

This work is often referred to as relating to body language but the participants were not taught to adjust their body language in the interview situation, they stood or sat differently for 2 minutes beforehand. They shifted their state and that state improved their performance.

A sense of connection and oxytocin

Another important hormone is oxytocin. Oxytocin and possibly endorphins[11] increase trust[12] and a sense of connection. Oxytocin also has an anti-stress and relaxation effect[13]. A way to increase oxytocin levels is to do "[...] self-massage, an activity that has been shown to lead to secretion of the hormone oxytocin, and the calm-and-connection response, which results in attenuation of arousal and stress levels."[14]

While this could be difficult to apply in the midst of a board meeting it is a simple and free method of self-care that can be applied in a quiet moment and could improve your performance by making you a better connecter – and therefore a better leader – to draw inspiration from Cuddy's article 'Connect, then lead'.

Cases of applying embodiment

The Leadership Embodiment method as specific example

Since I am trained as a certified Leadership Embodiment trainer / coach and know many people in that community I have taken the following specific examples from there. Leadership Embodiment was developed for use in businesses and organisations by Wendy Palmer. As with many of the other schools of embodiment, it developed out of the combination of Aikido, a Japanese martial art, and mindfulness, which itself comes out of Buddhism. During the last 30-40 years it has been refined for accessible and religion free use for professionals in organisations without any specific martial art or meditation background. It works with posture, breath and focus and teaches people how to influence their state of being with ease. The core of the practice is to recognize being in a stressful state and swiftly self-regulating into a flow-state. [Editor's Note – Clare Myatt describes similar practices elsewhere in this issue applied to working with addiction and trauma]

Case 1: Team dealing with stress from a re-organisation

Louise Robb[18] is a certified professional facilitator, for the case described she worked with an international NGO based in central Europe. It was part of a two-day team retreat with 30 people. Participants were doctors, specialists, managers, administration staff, all with at least a Masters degree. Purpose of the training was to deal with the stress that fast re-organisation had put on the faculty and to come to acceptance of the new situation. The embodiment part of the training consisted of half a day of Leadership Embodiment exercises like centering under pressure, exploring our survival patterns and how to benefit from these practices in everyday office situations.

Responses from participants were: "Wow. I feel strong and peaceful", "This is rubbish", and "In handling difficult situations it is not about developing skills to handle a situation, however more importantly is in managing ourselves and own emotions when in the face of conflict. This most insightful learning is the Aikido technique (Leadership Embodiment)."

On the subject of benefit of embodiment practice Louise remarks:

"I cannot do good work without it now."

"It's easy now to introduce, it was scary at first. It's backed by so much science and knowledge in the mainstream and if you can just get people to try, what they feel as a result speaks for itself.

In one organisation I have worked with over 1000 participants over the world and have feedback from them all about the two days we have the workshop and 80% remember the breathing and Aikido (their words for LE) saying they have shown their families and are using it every day at work to cope. It's only the very start for them, but it seems to make a big difference."

Case 2: Relational presence for coaches

Leanne Lowish[19] is a coaching supervisor trained in Leadership Embodiment. In this case she trained three groups of about ten self-selected coaches for the CSA (Coaching Supervision Academy) in two sessions of 2-4 hours. It was part of a piece on relational presence using embodiment techniques to explore what takes us out of being present and how to come back to presence. She used exercises on receiving criticism without taking it personally, a practice of gracefully interrupting, and leading and following.

A response from a participant was: "Find it enormously powerful".

The added benefit of embodiment practice according to Leanne:

"It's an excellent way of showing people how easily they are pulled out of presence and how simply they can come back. Also good for them to see their patterns and be able to identify them in their work with clients."

She notices it is easier nowadays to implement embodiment. The argument she uses mostly is around stress and how it pulls us out of thinking clearly and handling situations effectively.

Case 3: Teacher presence, inspiration, and connection

John Tuite[20] is an expert in teacher presence [Editor's Note – See John's excellent article in this volume]. In this case he worked in a state secondary school (11-18 years old) with four groups of five to eight newly qualified teachers of all subjects in their first year of teaching. The program consisted of two to three sessions of two hours long. This was part of a program which included a lesson observation with one to one feedback focused on the quality of presence, rather than specifically pedagogic strategies, followed up later in the year with a one-to one coaching session. Embodiment practices were used as a doorway into exploring presence, inspiration, and connection.

A specific exercise interesting for teachers is saying "no" in different ways, creating the distinction between a no that is definite, and a no that is both definite and connecting.

The added benefit of embodiment practice according to John:

"No other way to address these issues practically, rather than academically. Builds on their experience of being in the stressful conditions of a classroom. Acknowledges the different ways they respond to it, and offers them a way to work with it. Creates some distinctions that are not addressed anywhere else, but which are desperately needed."

With regards to making their case for embodiment in education John says:

"I don't use the word embodiment in selling this. I use 'presence'. I can discuss presence, but generally in terms of improving classroom management of behaviour. I talk about dealing with pressure, and the need for good teachers to be both strong and connected."

Conclusion

Embodiment is a maturing field that has much to offer to improve leadership, communication, and innovation in organisations. For decades it has been applied successfully in many businesses and organisations. The added value of the application of embodiment is supported by the recent increase in findings from neuroscience and psychology. The way we sit and stand changes the way we think , feel, and speak.

In today's busy work environments it doesn't take much to get triggered and having our amygdala reduce us to a more tense and self-centred version of ourselves. This has a negative effect on communication, employee morale, innovation, and company bottom-line. The solution to these problems is not to be found in more of the same knowledge-based training. It is advisable to implement an embodiment component in training and coaching, so employees can practice self-regulating their state of being. They can practice recognising, accepting, and adapting their physiological state and restore, even increase, their confidence, connection, and clarity.

It is important to understand that embodiment is a practice. We get better at applying the techniques in challenging situations, but we will fail. We cannot do it yet. This is to be expected, because the power is in the recovery. "Practice creates physiologically supported, embodied competency."[21]

Lastly I will indulge in a slightly utopian vision of cultivating enlightened business through incorporating embodiment practices. Naming embodiment as one of the practices that will help restore humanity in business, allowing capitalism to rise above itself and manifest its next stage of evolution: a conscious capitalism[22] with more humane work environments and a more enlightened society.

Bibliography

Anderson, E., Siegel, E. H., & Barrett, L. F. (2011). What you feel influences what you see: The role of affective feelings in resolving binocular rivalry. Journal of experimental social psychology, 47(4), 856-860.

Bohns, V. K., & Wiltermuth, S. S. (2012). It hurts when I do this (or you do that): Posture and pain tolerance. Journal of Experimental Social Psychology, 48(1), 341-345.

Brack, A.A. (2014). Insights on 3-D Leadership Development and Enactment

http://integralleadershipreview.com/11274-331-insights-3-d-leadership-development-enactment/ retrieved 28-08-2014

Brown, B. C. (2012). Leading complex change with post-conventional consciousness. Journal of Organizational Change Management, 25(4), 560-575.

Brown, Barrett C. Ph.D.: The Future of Leadership for Conscious Capitalism

https://associates.metaintegral.org/sites/default/files/MetaIntegral_B

rown_The%20future%20of%20leadership%20for%20conscious%20cap italism_20140402.pdf (accessed 01-09-2014)

Carney, D. R., Cuddy, A. J., & Yap, A. J. (2010). Power posing brief nonverbal displays affect neuroendocrine levels and risk tolerance. Psychological Science, 21(10), 1363-1368.

Carroll, B., Levy, L., & Richmond, D. (2008). Leadership as practice: challenging the competency paradigm. Leadership, 4(4), 363-379.

Cesario, J., & McDonald, M. M. (2013). Bodies in context: Power poses as a computation of action possibility. Social Cognition, 31(2), 260-274.

Crawford, J. (2011). The Brain-Friendly Organization: What Leadership Needs to Know for Intelligence to Flourish. http://www.cascadance.com/wp-content/uploads/2011/04/Crawford.Brain-Friendly-Organization.Article.Formatted.rev082911.pdf (Page 4 on Amygdala hijack, accessed 01-09-2014)

Cuddy, A. J., Wilmuth, C. A., & Carney, D. R. (2012). The benefit of power posing before a high-stakes social evaluation.

Cuddy, A. J., Kohut, M., & Neffinger, J. (2013). Connect, then lead. Harvard business review, 91(7), 54-61.

Dunbar, R. I. (2010). The social role of touch in humans and primates: behavioural function and neurobiological mechanisms. Neuroscience & Biobehavioral Reviews, 34(2), 260-268.

Fisher, K., & Robbins, C. R. (2014). Embodied leadership: Moving from leader competencies to leaderful practices. Leadership, 1742715014522680.

Hamill, P. (2011). Embodied leadership: towards a new way of developing leaders. Strategic HR Review, 10(5), 5-10.

Hermans, E. J., Putman, P., Baas, J. M., Koppeschaar, H. P., & Van Honk, J. (2006). A single administration of testosterone reduces fear-potentiated startle in humans. Biological psychiatry, 59(9), 872-874.

Kosfeld, M., Heinrichs, M., Zak, P. J., Fischbacher, U., & Fehr, E. (2005). Oxytocin increases trust in humans. Nature, 435(7042), 673-676.

Ladkin, D., & Taylor, S. S. (2010). Enacting the 'true self': Towards a theory of embodied authentic leadership. The Leadership Quarterly, 21(1), 64-74.

Lord, R. G., & Shondrick, S. J. (2011). Leadership and knowledge: Symbolic, connectionist, and embodied perspectives. The Leadership Quarterly, 22(1), 207-222.

Palmer, W. & Crawford, J. (2013). Leadership Embodiment, How the way we sit and stand can change the way we think and speak, ISBN 9781492946694

Walsh, Mark: The Science of Embodiment: Is There An Evidence-Base For Embodied Training? - http://integrationtraining.co.uk/blog/2013/03/science_of_embodiment.html (accessed 28-08-2014)

Park, L. E., Streamer, L., Huang, L., & Galinsky, A. D. (2013). Stand tall, but don't put your feet up: Universal and culturally-specific effects of expansive postures on power. Journal of Experimental Social

Psychology, 49(6), 965-971.

Siegel, D. J. (2009). Mindful awareness, mindsight, and neural integration. The Humanistic Psychologist, 37(2), 137-158.

Silsbee, D. (2013). Presence as Meta-Competency: Developing Leaders One Moment at a Time. Retrieved from http://www.dougsilsbee.com/pdf/metacompentency.pdf 28-08-2014

Stel, M., van Dijk, E., Smith, P. K., van Dijk, W. W., & Djalal, F. M. (2012). Lowering the pitch of your voice makes you feel more powerful and think more abstractly. Social Psychological and Personality Science, 3(4), 497-502.

Uvnäs-Moberg, K. E. R. S. T. I. N. (1996). Oxytocin linked antistress effects--the relaxation and growth response. Acta physiologica scandinavica. Supplementum, 640, 38-42.

Uvnäs-Moberg, K., Arn, I., & Magnusson, D. (2005). The psychobiology of emotion: the role of the oxytocinergic system. International journal of behavioral medicine, 12(2), 59-65.

Wilson AD and Golonka S (2013) Embodied cognition is not what you think it is. Front. Psychology 4:58. doi: 10.3389/fpsyg.2013.00058 - http://journal.frontiersin.org/Journal/10.3389/fpsyg.2013.00058/full (accessed 28-08-2014)

1Brief overview of Human Potential Movement: http://en.wikipedia.org/wiki/Human_Potential_Movement

2Wendy Palmer: Embodiment International http://www.embodimentinternational.com/

3Richard Strozzi-Heckler: Stozzi Institute http://www.strozziinstitute.com/

4Paul Linden: Being in Movement http://www.being-in-movement.com

5Personal Communication with Martin Saville: editor of *A Field Guide to Organisational Development: Taking Theory Into Practice*. (Griffin, M. E., Alsop, M. M., Saville, M. M., & Smith, M. G. (Eds.). (2014), and owner of http://www.mayvin.co.uk/

6Walsh, 2013

7Carney, 2010

8Cuddy, 2012

9Hermans, 2006

10Carney, 2010

11Dunbar, 2010

12Kosfeld, 2005

13Uvnäs-Moberg, 1996

14Uvnäs-Moberg, 2005

15Crawford, 2011

16Palmer, 2014

17Siegel, 2009

18Louise H. Robb – www.louiserobb.co.uk – Facilitation, Leadership Embodiment / leadership development, coaching team / coaching individual, practice development groups.

19Leanne Lowish - Director and Programme Leader at Coaching Supervision Academy Asia Pacific and UK - www.coachingsupervisionacademy.com - Leadership, teams and culture change facilitator at Axialent - www.axialent.com

20John Tuite – www.centreforembodiedwisdom.com - Leadership development and somatic coaching, educational consultancy, and teacher of embodied awareness and mind and body integration.

21Doug Silsbee, 2013

22Brown, 2014

Printed in Great Britain
by Amazon

36101457R00056